# Water Torture

by  Dean Forêt

# Chapter One
## Don't vote. It just encourages them

Friday, March 31, 2000

2:57 p.m.

Part of me wanted to ask the headline-grabbing question, part of me
wanted to run all the way home.

My hands were sticky with sweat. From a far corner on the
Opposition side of the provincial Legislature, I perched on the edge
of my seat, watching the Speaker. As a punk chick, I sat where the
good ol' boys had put me--as far from the Speaker's throne as
possible, barely inside the House. At this distance, any Liberal in a
suit could more easily catch Mr. Speaker's eye. Yet, I thought, if I
could just get the floor, there might be time for me get in one little
question.

"Order!"

Wiping sweaty palms on the Woolly One, my only semi-respectable
skirt, I checked the clock on the wall. Two minutes to go. Taking a
deep relaxing breath, my lungs took in a toxic perfume stew of
creaky leather, waxed floors, fear and testosterone.

"O-r-der!"

In the British parliamentary tradition, legislators enjoy the unfettered
right to freedom of speech; that's why sometimes the guys all seem
to talk at once, and why nobody can hear what anyone else is saying.
Another rule is that only one member stands at a time and, if he can
hold his ground while others are trying to shout him down, he is said
to "have the floor." When the Speaker, who is supposed to referee
this free-for-all, gets to his feet or "takes the floor," every other
legislator is supposed to sit down and shut up.

"Order!!"

Speaker Woo shook an unwelcome wrinkle from the silk sleeve of his barrister's robes and craned up to his full six feet, six inches. The part-time pages on the steps below Woo's throne followed him to their feet. The pages, all high-school honour-roll nerds, fidgeted in their regulation velvet knee breeches and buckled shoes, while Woo appealed for calm with the upheld palms of his bony hands.

"Order!"

The clock ticked. One minute to go. Question Period was dying a noisy, painful death. To my right, a frontbench Liberal heckled the Minister of Housing. The minister laughed, and up in the press gallery a reporter yawned. Standing again, the Liberal showily stuffed files in his briefcase and momentarily blocked my view of the speaker.

Come on, Woo. If you let me, I can still beat the clock.

As legislators on both sides of the House gathered their papers and stole away one by one through the lobbies to "meetings" in nearby bars, my dreams of parliamentary stardom faded. Only a bare quorum remained, a dozen suits lashed to their seats by the party whips. My target, Daniel D. Lyon, buttoned his jacket, shot his cuffs and stood up. "Dandy," please don't go, I thought. I want some time with you.

Thirty seconds.

"Order." The speaker's thin fingers picked at the hem of his robe until something like quiet returned to the Chamber, then he lowered himself into his seat. The pages followed Woo, moving down to their seats on the steps below his throne. "Order, please! One last question. A short one."

Being pink and petite confers no advantages in a prairie legislature, so I shot to my feet with my hand held high and yelled, "Mr. Speaker! Mr. Speaker!"

Woo's eyes slowly inspected the Opposition ranks. He looked past my waving hand, considered a nearby Independent's pleading look, then, deciding perhaps that I was the lesser of two evils, he reluctantly gave me the floor. "The Mem-ber for West-side."

I tucked white shirt into woolly skirt and, with exaggerated deference, bowed at the chair—the throne rather than Woo. "Mr. Speaker, I have a question for the Minister of Housing and Municipal Affairs."

The Minister of Agriculture, A. B. Plumb, looked up, then with a heavy hand he restrained the departing Lyon. Normally, I hated Plumb, a used-car dealer famous for his bad breath and barnyard humour, but for that brief moment he was my friend.

Lyon slid back into his seat as Plumb nodded his fat purple nose in my direction. A hard-looking man with pockmarked cheeks, Lyon muttered something into a cupped hand and winked at Plumb, then the Tory troops hunkered down to guard the Treasury against this last-minute attack.

"A question for the Minister of Housing."

I paused for a second while the television cameras sought me out. As the lenses focused on my seat, a gaggle of New Democrats gathered round to cheer my raid on the provincial piggy bank. Hightucker, Carlson and Maurice filled in the empty seats to my right and in front so those innocents at home, watching cable television, might think I was addressing a full House. Cable viewers would see the theatre not the reality of a half-empty legislature. Hightucker, my seatmate, urged me on, "Go for it, Reggie!"

I pounced on Lyon. "Mr. Speaker, every day we all pass a young beggar who sleeps outside on the stone-cold steps of this Legislature in nothing but a ragged army overcoat. Even after six calls to Social Services on her behalf…she sits there still."

The ministers of agribusiness and condominiums greeted this preamble with barely muffled snorts. Taking their cue from the ministers, the Tory backbenchers weighed in with their own mocking grunts. Fixing my eyes on a vanishing point beyond my notes, I paused until the tittering ended, then lifted my head.

"Within ten city blocks of this chamber, we see dozens like her--street kids, former mental patients and bag ladies."

"Take them all your house, why don't you?" Lyon sneered. Plumb slapped his knee and hee-hawed like a Disney donkey.

Dropping my notes, I turned on Lyon. "It is sad that the Minister of Housing finds the homeless so funny--especially since he is the one person here who could help them."

Plumb wagged a finger at me; Lyon merely shifted slightly in his seat.

"Here is my question: Will the Minister of Housing agree that this province's homeless urgently need a new low-income public-housing program?"

Lyon studied the shine on his boots for a long, considered moment before stepping into the aisle beside his desk. He hooked his thumbs in the waistband of his trousers and trotted out his overbearing-male act. "The member must know that last year this province broke the record for housing starts. Private developers do a fantastic job, and I see no reason to interfere in their good work."

Figuring he'd shut me down, Lyon slid back into his seat. Plumb slapped his back, as if Lyon had just won the agriculture ministry's prize for Best Bull.

"Supplementary," Woo injected.

"The homeless folk will be overjoyed to know what a great job the developers are doing for them," I shot back. "Perhaps the minister will tell us why his Government and his golfing buddy, the mayor, allow the demolition of perfectly sound old apartment blocks in the core area of the capital city to make room for luxury hotels and condominiums? Where does he think the residents of the old blocks are going to live? On the streets?"

"Stupid cunt," I heard Plumb grumble, and the government backbenchers snickered. I considered a protest, but tomorrow's Hansard would of course contain no record of this insult;

parliamentarians are not allowed to call each other "stupid."

But I let it go. With an eye on the Speaker, I pressed on, lifting my voice over the commotion. "Why doesn't this government insist that developers make some apartments available to low-income families in this city? Why doesn't the Provincial Housing Corporation build replacement housing? Why doesn't this government establish any emergency shelters for the homeless? Why, why, why?"

Lyon rolled his eyes. "Because, young lady, we have no money in the budget for that kind of thing. Wake up to the New Reality."

"The Minister of Housing asks, 'Where's the money?' The age-old cry of the right-winger looking for an excuse to ignore a human need. Mr. Speaker, I'll tell you where the money is. This province provides big-time tax incentives and loan guarantees for developers to put up chain hotels and convention centres. Why not guarantee loans to local builders to build affordable housing for our own citizens?"

"The market knows best," Plumb heckled from his seat, his cheeks colouring.

"Why not?" I shouted over him.

Woo leaned forward in his throne, ready to cut me off. "It costs less to build an apartment unit than a hotel room. Today, we have vacant hotel rooms all over town, but hardly any affordable apartments. Imagine that: clean, comfortable rooms sitting empty while human beings bed down on icy sidewalks."

Lyon shook his head in mock sadness.

"Imagine that!" I demanded of Lyon.

Plumb huffed and puffed, then blew me a raspberry.

"Or-der, order." Woo started to unfold his skeletal frame.

I leaned forward, almost pleading now. "Doesn't the minister give a damn for the poor and homeless?"

In this jibe, Lyon must have thought he heard a tabloid headline and tensed, ready to beat it or make me eat it. The minister planted his knuckles in the leather of his seat and bowed his head. Ready and set. With a pointed finger, Plumb fired imaginary bullets at my head, while his troops cheered each hit.

Woo stood.

I was almost done, but, foolishly, I couldn't resist one last shot. "The Minister of Housing should remember we were elected to help other people, not to help ourselves!"

Lyon's eyes flashed, and he stepped into the aisle, shouting at the chair. "Mr. Speaker, a question of privilege. Question of privilege!"

Woo sighed audibly. "As all members know, in this House a genuine question of privilege takes precedence over all other business. The speaker must hear the complaint, then determine if there's a legitimate case. So, I recognize the Minister of Housing on a question of privilege."

I settled back, helpless to stop this manoeuvre. In the parliamentary game known locally as Pitching Woo, I knew already that Lyon, a grandmaster of plastic emotion, rarely failed to get the Speaker's jaded ear.

"If that member is hinting that I have my hand in the till," Lyon roared, "she had better make a specific charge or withdraw the remark."

The Tories shouted, "Withdraw! Withdraw!"

Fixing his eyes on Woo, Lyon growled, "I'm sure Mr. Speaker will affirm: if the Member for Westside fails to prove her charge, she will have to resign her seat!"

As if he'd been wounded in battle, Lyon lowered himself gently into his seat. Slyly, like a soccer faker, out of the corner of his eye, he watched referee Woo consider his complaint.

When I got a free moment I resolved to analyze Lyon's game. Lyon was no fool. He was not just the housing minister; he was also the Tories' political minister in this city. Perhaps I'd accidentally hit a nerve. Whatever. By the simple device of changing the subject, he'd succeeded nicely in deflecting my attack on behalf of the homeless. Damn him.

The speaker rubbed his eyes then summoned the clerk to advise him on the correct procedure. Easing his chair away from the table in the centre aisle, the cuddly old clerk tugged sharply at his waistcoat and tiptoed up to touch the Speaker's silky elbow.

As the House officers huddled, I glanced around and happened to notice a uniformed cop push open the main doors to the chamber. The cop was a large man with a face like a lumpy seed potato. Nudging my seatmate's arm, I fingered the intruder.

Hightucker called out. "Stranger in the House!"

The cop paused inside the entrance just before the Bar of the House and carefully removed his cap.

Everybody shifted their attention from the Speaker to the stranger. Like kids in a playground, members on all sides began to chant: "Stranger! Stranger!"

Surprised to find himself the focus of so much attention, the cop stood there, cap in hand, his eyes darting from one side of the House to the other.

Reporters picked up their pens, and the sergeant-at-arms looked up from his crossword puzzle, a rare event in itself. The sergeant limped stiffly towards the bar to halt the intruder's advance.

"Out!" The sergeant barked. With one white-gloved hand on the hilt of his ceremonial sword, he marched towards the constable.

"But…" The cop opened his mouth in protest, but the sergeant would hear none of it. Without another word, the sergeant shooed him out of the chamber.

A page followed the puzzled cop through the double doors and returned seconds later with a report for the Sergeant, who then got up to pass it on to the Clerk--the chain of command a-clanking.

The speaker conferred with the clerk and the sergeant for a minute then dismissed them both with a swipe of his Order Paper. In a singsong voice, Woo invited me to defend myself. "The Mem-ber for Westside. On the question of privilege."

Stumped, I wiped my hands on Woolly One. "I withdraw, Mr. Speaker."

Woo bowed deeply in my direction, then sat. The majority thumped their desks, cheering Lyon's little victory.

"My apologies to the Minister," I said, then added, "I did not intend to imply that he was a thief, only that he should open his heart and his mind to the less fortunate."

Slumping back into my seat, I shot a mournful glance at Hightucker, who replied with a funereal smile.

Lyon rose again to press his advantage.

"Finish her off," Plumb whispered.

Lyon smiled magnanimously. "One last point, on the question of privilege, Mr. Speaker. The Honourable Member won't mind if I quote Winston Churchill's observation that, 'a fanatic is someone who can't change her mind and won't change the subject.'"

"Watch it, Reggie," Hightucker whispered out of the side of his mouth.

I spotted the trap--but too late. By standing again, I'd already put my foot in it.

Woo waved me on with the Order Paper.

An uncustomary hush awaited my response. Bowing gracelessly to the chair, I turned again to face Lyon. "Actually, Churchill said a fanatic is someone who won't change <u>his</u>mind."

For a split second, silence reigned in the chamber, then the tension broke and laughter crossed the floor. For the first time, my claque applauded spontaneously. Members on all sides actually smiled, Woo covered his mouth and even Lyon conceded the point with a curt nod.

"Perhaps the Minister of Housing agrees with former President Reagan that people who sleep on sidewalks are 'homeless by choice,'" I offered politely and sat down. This remark brought cheers from both sides of the House: for Reagan on the one, for Regina on the other. But the momentum was mine again.

Woo rattled the paper in his hand. "The Member for Westside's questions have been somewhat wordy today, but, because she is relatively new to this place, I will grant her one final supplementary question."

You condescending prick, I thought. Peeking at the wall clock, I realized that technically Question Period was long gone. A page appeared at my side with a message. Scanning it quickly, I saw the words: "Urgent. Please call the coroner." What the hell was this? Dad? Got to get out of here. Fast.

The speaker opened his eyes and blinked at me. "Does the Mem-ber for Westside want a final supplementary or not?"

I considered my options. Hightucker could not take over my question. If I surrendered the floor it might be a week before I'd get another chance. Quickly, I scanned my crib sheets, but could not find my place.

Woo broke the silence with a stagy cough. Every eye in the House watched me clumsily sort through my script.

"United Nation's housing studies show that without something approaching security of tenure…" With my head down, I charged through the text, racing through rhetoric and statistics, as if this were my maiden address--and my last.

"Faster," Lyon taunted. "Faster!"

"Could you repeat that?" Plumb heckled.

"Faster!"

To hell with them all, I thought.

The Tories banged their desks triumphantly as I raced off the floor.

Hightucker called out to me as I fled, but I did not look back.

Outside a pack of reporters lay in wait. They sprang at me as the doors parted, yapping all at once. "Regina! Regina! Aren't you staying for the answer to your question?"

"What's the name of the homeless woman?"

"Was the cop here to see you?"

"Where are you going now?"

I pushed past them, running now as I crossed the rotunda. The news hounds sped up. But I outran them.

As I reached the elevators, a hairy hand in a corduroy sleeve grabbed my arm. "Hey Regina, just friend to friend, what's up?"

I glanced at my only friend among the reporters. "Can't stop now, Moss. Something urgent." I stepped into the elevator marked Members Only. When the doors closed, I reread the slip in my quivering hand. "Ms. Colwell. Urgent. Please call the coroner." The message had come from a Dr. Corbeau.

I charged into the caucus office with the message clutched in my hand.

"What does the coroner want, Heather?"

In that unique accent her workmates had labelled "skittish," Heather breathlessly chased the words out of her mouth. "I cannot say, love, and I had the man on the line, yet he would no wait, but do you want me to ring him now?"

"Didn't he tell you anything? It's not Dad, is it?"

"Not a word, but I'm sure he would have said if it was a family matter." Heather gave my arm a quick, comforting squeeze.

I took a deep breath. "I'll make the call. Give me a minute, okay, Heather?"

"Surely. You have the number." Heather pointed to the paper in my hand. "I can stay, if you want me to."

"It's okay."

"I'll be out in the hall."

I sank into the warm, cushioned swivel chair behind my aide's desk and pecked out the number. While the phone rang, my eyes tracked over the framed photographs on the opposite wall. My ballet company, my graduating class and my party caucus: all advertising, I now realized, Regina Colwell's desperate need to belong.

"Apartment Hotel," sang a breathless soprano.

"Sorry, I must have the wrong number."

"Who are you trying to reach, Madam?"

I glanced again at the message. "Extension 505."

"With whom did you wish to speak, Madam?"

"The coroner. Dr. Corbeau."

"I'm sorry but that line is busy now. Please hold."

Recorded music filled my ear. It took a few seconds before the lyric sunk in, then Madonna stopped singing "Daddy," and the call rang through. A gruff male voice answered, "Yes?"

"The coroner, please."

Seconds passed while some men talked in the background, then someone with a stuffy nose picked up the telephone. "Corbeau here," he sniffed.

"It's Regina Colwell, Doctor. You called my office?"

Corbeau sneezed explosively. "Ms. Colwell, I'll come straight to the point. I'm downtown at the Apartment Hotel. I think it's part of your constituency."

"Just inside my boundaries." Constituency, not family. I loosened my grip on the phone. "What's the problem?"

"Well, I have a dead youth here, and I think you may know him."

"A young man? What's his name?" I swallowed my breath.

"Water. Norman Water. Is he, by chance, a friend of yours?"

# Chapter Two
## Pay now or pay later; it's later than you think

Friday, March 31

4:39 p.m.

Even for a rookie legislator in a swing constituency, I was thinking, fourteen blocks is a long way to walk, just to meet a dead elector.

In the narrow flower bed bordering The Apartment Hotel parking lot, dirty brown willow bushes squatted in the snow banks and a pair of scraggy pines reached for the sky. Up against the front wall and along the driveway, snowdrifts thawed in the setting sun, resurrecting from beneath the grubby slush last year's Cheezie wrappers and the mud that would soon be summer dust. I tried to remember if ever I had canvassed this poll.

The Apartment Hotel seemed a deliberately ambiguous name. Was it an apartment, a hotel or both? High-rise apartment blocks in poorer neighbourhoods could be the death of constituency politicians. They were normally the natural habitat of singles, transients, television junkies, sometime voters--all decidedly Undecided and notoriously susceptible to national trends. Approximately four hundred of those rootless, disconnected individuals, who parallel parked in the elevators and passed each other heads-down in the hallways, lived here--more than enough to ditch my political dreams.

Was my late constituent, Norman Water, one of these enigmas? Had I ever talked with him? I didn't think so. So why did the coroner need me to identify him? Why me? It might be my constituency, but it was border country, a zone of perpetual political skirmishing. I was a something of a stranger here and did not feel completely at home.

Out front, a tourist coach, a panel truck and an ambulance sat bumper to bumper, blocking the doorway. As I glanced northwards, an icy blast of Arctic air whipped my hair around my face and made my eyes weep. I clambered over the truck's trailer hitch, used the pebbled rubber mat to wipe grit off the soles of my Doc Martens and pushed through the airtight doors.

What had once been the cramped entrance area of a low-rent apartment block was in the process of becoming the claustrophobic lobby of an instant hotel. Sawdust and varnish vapours polluted the air. Plastic sheets shrouded the lobby furniture. Carpenters gunned nails into plywood, and electric saws screamed through two-by-fours. Over the din, a deathly pale salesman shouted orders into the lobby pay phone. From stereo speakers in the false ceiling, Madonna pitched "Material Girl" to the men below. Leaning in like a preacher at the altar, an elderly female desk clerk worked a cash register at the check-in counter. Beneath the counter, a penitent painter kneeled to touch-up the trim.

Across the lobby, standing by an open elevator, was the cop who had invaded the Legislature during Question Period. I walked past the carpenters and painters towards the elevator. The desk clerk momentarily glanced up from her work as I went by. Nobody else gave me a second look.

I offered the cop my politician's hand. He studied it for a second before picking it up with clumsy delicacy, as he might in bagging a piece of evidence. Shoving Exhibit A into my pocket, I boarded the elevator.

The doors closed, and the cop looked at the ceiling.

"I'm sorry."

He ignored me.

"About this afternoon." I thought that he might be pouting. Were cops allowed to pout? "Only elected members and the clerk's staff are allowed on the floor when the legislative assembly is sitting."

The cop looked at me sideways. He thought I was mocking him.

"Even police officers?"

"Especially police officers."

He challenged me with a full-frontal pout.

"It's a long story, going back to the English Civil War."

"English?"

"Yeah, the famous one--in America--came later. Back in 1641, King Charles tried to arrest some of his critics in Parliament, and that led to a civil war. Ever since, the Crown's representatives have to get an invitation before entering a parliament. Like when the Governor General reads the Speech from the Throne."

The cop screwed up his face, took a deep breath and pinched his nostrils between his thumb and forefinger.

Not interested. This western lawman wanted no history lessons from some young skirt.

The elevator doors opened, and the stink enveloped us. Holding my breath, I followed the cop down the hall past a long line of numbered doorways. Number 505 was open a crack, and I heard voices inside. With one hand holding his nose, the constable used the other to push the door open, then to steer me through it.

I stood at the threshold gagging at the stench. The police had cranked the windows wide open in the tiny one-room apartment, but Number 505 still stank. They had also liberally distributed Lysol around the apartment but the disinfectant could do nothing to disguise the insistent odour of shit and piss and rotting meat. Whatever my sins, I did not want to be in this place.

The walls were grey with grime and graffiti, except for two pale patches where a couch and a television had once stood. A long wall by the kitchen was covered in rows and rows of pencilled hieroglyphics. Not an arm or leg of furniture remained. Someone had mopped the kitchen floor, I noticed, but the carpet was still decorated with a bizarre collage of overlapping stains.

Out on the balcony, a couple of ambulance attendants in white parkas shared a joke and a smoke. They stopped laughing when I entered, but gave me only a quick once-over before turning back to their cigarettes and the sight of an orange sun setting into the dark clouds gathering on the western horizon.

Over by the open window, a balding man in a navy blue ski jacket and baggy grey slacks dabbed his nose with a damp tissue as he talked on the phone. Mister Pouting Potato Face stood by with his back to me and his hand over his mouth. When the phone call was done, the cop touched the sleeve of the blue ski jacket. The balding man looked up and smiled in my direction. He had black bags under his eyes, which made him look very sad.

Gently, he set the phone down onto the floor. "Miss Colwell, thanks for coming on such short notice. I'm Dr. Lee Corbeau. You may remember me. I ran for the House of Commons in this district back in '68." With that, Corbeau grabbed my hand with both of his, as if we'd been comrades in some old war.

"You're talking about the Trudeau landslide, right?"

He laughed. "A bad year for the Tories."

"I came of age under Reagan and Thatcher, the good years."

"How stupid of me. Of course." He sneezed into his hand.

I handed him a Kleenex from my pocket.

"Thanks. Does the smell bother you?" he asked. "With this darn cold, I hardly notice it. Anyway, I'm rather used to it after all these years."

"You're a political appointee then?" I realized, now, the meaning of what he'd said earlier about the Trudeau landslide.

The doctor sniffed. "Let me assure you: I'm qualified and completely professional. Still, if you'd rather talk to the constable alone, that will be fine with me."

I glanced at the cop, then studied the saggy bags under Corbeau's eyes and the nose that he had rubbed to a raw redness. "That's okay."

He sniffed again. "I suppose you know my role in a case like this?"

"Not exactly."

"Well...."Corbeau looked around the room for a place to deposit his used Kleenex. "When a person dies in an accident, or in some unusual circumstance, the police call me to the scene. After examining the body, I may order an autopsy. In this city a pathologist at the University Hospital does the honours. When the pathologist reports, I have to decide whether to hold an inquest. If we proceed with an inquest, then the coroner's jury brings in a verdict on the cause of death." Corbeau finally stuffed the sodden Kleenex into his shirt pocket.

"I see."

"That's the exception. In most cases, as coroner, I have the last word. Is that clear enough?"

"Crystal. Now I know what you're doing here. What about me?"

"Do you mind if we ask you some questions?"

"No."

"The constable here will take his own notes. Okay, Spud?" Cool, I thought. I was not the only one who thought the cop resembled a root vegetable.

The constable pulled a notebook out of his pocket and unbuttoned the strap to release his pen.

"This interview will provide some background for my report. That's all. No need to fret about it," Corbeau added. "This is not a criminal matter yet."

"Fine," I said.

"Well, as I told you on the phone, we have a dead boy here."

"Norman Water?" I swallowed my breath.

Corbeau looked up. "Right. Norman Water. You know his name?"

"You told me. On the phone."

"So, do you know him?"

"No."

"The name Norman Water doesn't mean anything to you?"

"No, nothing at all."

"Not professionally, or privately? No relationship whatsoever?"

"Relationship?"

"Friend, relative…lover?"

"No."

The coroner studied my face. He seemed to be examining my complexion for the tiniest of flaws. "You have men in your life?"

I nodded.

Spud interrupted. "Many men?"

I turned on him. "What the hell do you mean by that?"

Corbeau tried to calm me. "Perhaps you just don't remember Norman. Is that possible?"

"No." I returned his gaze, but when he snatched up the used Kleenex to dab at his nose, I flinched. At that moment, two hotel cleaners with buckets and scrubbing brushes arrived. They paused at the door until Corbeau gave them the go-ahead. "Just the walls for now."

I looked over at the graffiti and the hieroglyphics. "Isn't that evidence?"

Spud laughed at my curiosity. "We have Polaroids."

Corbeau sniffed. "Let me introduce you to the victim, then we can talk some more." Taking me by the wrist, he led me towards the bathroom. I followed slowly, but followed just the same.

The coroner opened the door, hopped over a puddle on the linoleum and swept back the shower curtain. Between the surface scum and the dregs visible on the murky bottom of the half-filled bathtub lay a naked and emaciated corpse.

At one glance, I took in the soft brown whiskers on the hollow white cheeks, the exposed ribs and the greasy hair, even the shrunken penis. But I couldn't look twice at the staring sea-green eyes. He was so goddamned young, so goddamned dead. I had a momentary thought of the crucified Christ and felt inexplicable guilt. Grabbing the doorknob for support, I turned away.

"Never saw him before?"

I shook my head. "No."

Corbeau gave me a sceptical look. "Bear with me for a moment." He grabbed the corpse by the wrist and twisted it sharply upwards. "Here." He turned up the dead hand for me to see.

I learned forward, tentatively. Scum slopped around the rim of the bathtub.

"Look." Corbeau insisted.

In blurred purple ink, on the terrible wrinkled whiteness of Norman Water's right palm were my name and phone number.

# Chapter Three
# Do do me, Madonna.

Friday, March 31

6:16 p.m.

I watched the ambulance attendants strap down the corpse, pack the stretcher into the hall, then turn it upright so that it would fit inside the elevator. The coroner, the cop and the attendants flanking the body beckoned me to join them for the ride. I took half a step forward then balked momentarily until a party of tourists rounded the corner and crowded me onto the elevator. The doors closed on the tourists, Norman Water's entourage and me. Propping myself in a corner, I pulled the collar of my leather jacket around my ears and hugged myself tight.

Oblivious to the body on board—and its foul odour--a tiny manic tourist provided a running commentary to his fellow travellers as he monitored the illuminated numbers on the control panel. "Outside, it's three below on the metric scale. How cold is that, anyway? I don't think we'll be warm enough in these coats. Fourth floor. The travel agent should have warned us. Wait until I see those fools. Pow! We'd better not have to wait long for a taxi, or it'll be World War Three! Third Floor. Do they have Yellow Cab around here? They're number one, the best. We'll get the front desk to call Yellow. Did you see on the TV news that Quebec Province wants to join up with France? Second Floor. I think they're nuts."

With a polite Canadian bow, I waved the visitors and stretcher-bearers through the door. Traversing the lobby towards the front door, I stepped carefully over snakes of electric cable under ladders and around plywood stacks. The carpenters and plumbers were packing up for the day. At the lobby entrance, I stood and watched as the attendants loaded Norman into the ambulance. The construction crew followed them out, slammed doors and drove off.

I did not move; there was nowhere I wanted to go.

Snow flew about the darkening streets outside the lobby. A gentle dusting of white frost to ice the winter cake might be okay, I thought, but spare me this freaky tempest with its slashing winds and icy crystals slicing up the night. For several minutes I watched the snow slanting left to right, then the wind shifted, and some flakes spattered the glass doors. The flakes melted on impact and dribbled down the pane. Sealed against the storm outside, yet trapped in this half-finished fake hotel, I felt my mood darkening. I could feel the black night lurking at the back of my brain, one of those little bipolar lows that sometimes dogged my days.

The tourists gathered at the counter while the clerk phoned for a taxi.

"Not red, not green, Yellow," Manic Man insisted.

"Twenty minutes, minimum, sorry," said the desk clerk.

Muttering about the Canadian weather and the national taxi shortage, the tourists adjourned to The Oasis Saloon off the lobby.

Shivering slightly, I lowered myself onto the plastic sheet covering the armchair by the front entrance and stared out through the glass doors, my mind wandering into the storm. Why would a dying boy write my name and number on his hand? As far as I knew, he had been a complete stranger--certainly not the kind of stray male that, even in my wild days, I sometimes used to take back to my place. Who the hell was Norman Water, anyway? Where did he come from? How, and why, did he die?

The coroner had explained his legal obligation to investigate the young man's death. He'd even promised to call me first thing Monday if he had anything to report. It struck me now that Corbeau had told me diddly squat about Norman Water and absolutely nothing of what he suspected might be the cause of the kid's untimely end. When I asked Corbeau why Norman had died, all he offered was, "Can't say yet." I probably should not hold my breath waiting for Corbeau's call.

Sitting straight up in the chair, I decided that I really ought to find my way home through the storm to my apartment. But, I realized I just couldn't face the long march home, or indeed the whole unhealthy scene there. Unfortunately for me, an unwelcome guest had taken over my apartment. Moss.

Moss claimed to be both a friend and a neighbour but had recently given me plenty of reasons to doubt him on both counts. As much as any reporter ever befriends a politician, Moss probably qualified as a friend and, so far as apartment dwellers ever really become neighbours, he came fairly close, living as he did just down the hall. So, when his partner, Robyn, showed him the door, Moss had begged good old Regina to let him camp at my place, just for "a night or two." Reluctantly, I had agreed. Just an overnight visitor, I had told myself. Now I couldn't get rid of the guy.

I'm never sure about Moss. He comes on pretty strong sometimes but maybe he does that with every chick he meets. If he's a habitual hit man and comes on to every woman equally, I could handle that. But if he's got the serious hots for my body, then, it's not so cool. He's at least ten years too old and way too flower power to fit into my limited and workbound life. Besides, bedding reporters and pissing-off girlfriends are two things which are just not on my agenda.

Right now, the relentless reporter and his ex-girlfriend were two problems I needed like a snap election right now. What I wanted was a retreat, an escape from both domestic stress and political wars, a temporary hideaway, time to repair my black mood. One more night in the apartment with Moss, and I might do something I'd regret.

Wrapped in my biker jacket, with one Doc Marten planted neatly beside the other, I slouched in the lobby chair, busily convincing myself that even now I might do some good for Norman Water. In fact, this hotel was a perfect example of what I had been talking about in my question, the replacement of housing stock by hotel rooms. By staying put I might be able to research my constituent's plight. Maybe I could learn something of Norman's life in this place. Maybe I could play let's pretend. Pretend that I needed a place to stay the night. Pretend that the Apartment Hotel perfectly met my current needs. Anything was possible, and isn't politics the art of the possible, I was thinking--when some terribly pained Queen's English breached my private musings.

"Good evening, Madam. Don't mind my asking, but are you a guest of the hotel?"

I raised my eyes to find a huge woman in a dinner jacket and very shiny black pumps closing in on me. She was well over six feet tall and very broad-shouldered, with slicked-back hair and a regal but ponderous manner. Everything about the woman was instantly alarming, from her muscle builder's gait to her imperious accent.

"I'm very sorry to trouble you," the heavy said through stiff lips, "but are you a guest of the hotel?" Her whole manner seemed absurd, as if she thought this dump belonged to Donald Trump.

Somewhat disoriented, I had trouble connecting my mouth to my brain. I was mindful of the Apartment Hotel both as it was and as it had become. "I am thinking of getting an apartment--just for the night."

"Apart-ment?" The heavy repeated the word as if to savour the sound or, perhaps, to correct my pronunciation. I became even more confused. She was acting like some deposed monarch, now suddenly slumming on the Canadian prairies.

"Apartment? Not exactly, I'd like a room for the night."

"Ah, I see. Yes. Does Madam have any luggage with her?" The heavy pointedly surveyed both sides of the chair. "Are your bags in the lobby? Behind the front desk? In storage?"

With thick manicured fingers, the woman drew back the flap of her dinner jacket. For god's sake, now she was showing off her shoulder holster!

"No, not here," I had actually begun to stammer.

"Where then?" The woman was polished and polite but slightly off-putting.

"At home."

She inhaled noisily and clapped her right hand into her left. Once. A right-handed hitter. "And where--if you don't mind my asking--is home?"

"You want my address?"

She slapped her fist into the palm of her free hand. "I'm really sorry to have to ask this but where . . . do . . . you . . . live?"

"Here," I waved out at the storm.

She nodded, once. "Of course. Then why on earth don't you go home, Madam? If I may be so bold as to ask."

Pushing myself up by the arms of the chair, I forced her to take two steps backwards. "Not that it's anyone's business, but I don't own a car, and no buses are running."

For the first time, I looked straight into the woman's eyes, and the eyes looked back, glassy and blank, like marbles. From the overpowering stench, I guessed she'd washed her face in Brut.

"One could wait hours for a taxi," I said with a phoney English accent.

The heavy appeared not to notice. "Ah, hah! So, Madam is waiting for taxi? You want a taxi, right?"

"Not exactly. As I said, I thought about getting a room . . . for the night."

"Oh, really." The big woman's hand found the small of my back and steered me to the front counter. The counter was now plastic-wrapped like the rest of the lobby furniture. Addressing the clerk, she asked. "Lily, are we full?"

The clerk, an older woman in a frilly white blouse, looked frightened, as if she'd no idea how to deal with the question. Her eyes darted from my face to the bouncer's, then back. Lily bowed her head. "Do you have a reservation?" she asked me.

A skill-testing question. Answer the question and win the prize, a weekend the Apartment Hotel. I searched for a clue in the clerk's face, but Lily turned away rather than look me in the eye.

"You do have a reservation?" Lily pleaded.

"I do?" My eyes shifted from the ruffled clerk to the overdressed heavy.

"You do?"

"Do I?" I pleaded ignorance with my hands.

The heavy was not amused. She looked down her nose at me and in a queenly voice, asked, "Do . . . you . . . have . . . a . . . reservation?"

"Don't think so."

"Do you perhaps have a credit card?"

"Hell, no."

The regal female stared down at me. "No cards?"

"Don't believe in them."

"Not one?"

"I have plenty of cash. See." For the clerk's benefit, I reached into the pocket of my leather jacket, pulled out my wallet and started to open the billfold. But before I could show her the money, the heavy grabbed my arm. "Not one credit card?"

"No."

"What, might I ask, are you doing here?"

I looked at the flint in her eyes, her grim appraisal of my studded leather jacket, my Docs, my lack of make-up. I didn't fit any of her rigid categories of woman. Sometimes though, I should just bite my tongue because I am a bit too mouthy for my own good.

"I'm a hooker."

My inquisitor's lips stiffened, and her hand came up to smooth the hair on her scalp, then she jumped to a conclusion. "You're out of here." Grabbing my jacket at the collar, she started dragging me towards the door. "On your way."

"Let me go!" I yelled and twisted out of the heavy's reach. The tourists poured out of the bar to watch the fuss, and I retreated a few steps until my back touched the counter. "You really think I look like a sex worker, do you?"

Furious, I flipped open my wallet again and waved it at the giant. "Do you see that? That's an ID card. My name is Regina Colwell, Member of the Legislative Assembly for this district. I'm a political pro--not a prostitute."

The heavy reached for her shoulder holster, unbuttoned the flap and pulled out a pager. She stared at the pager, looking for some signal, checked its power switch, then replaced it in the holster. At a loss for words, she just didn't know what to do next.

The tourists were gawking at me, so I turned my back on them, and put away my wallet. Having to produce an identity card in my own constituency was truly humiliating. So much for my name recognition.

"Excuse me," I addressed the clerk, "Is there any adult supervision around here? Like, do you have a boss?"

Lily froze.

"Where the hell is your manager?!"

The heavy idly stretched her neck inside her collar, as if confrontations like this only made her day, then reached forward to draw me away from my tourist audience. "I am the assistant general manager. My name is Queenie De Lis." She offered me a thick fist.

"What do you do here?"

Queenie folded her arms across her substantial chest. "Assistant general manager."

"That's your title; what do you do?"

Queenie pinched her nose. "As the general factotum, I lend the establishment a little class."

"I can see that."

"Excellent!"

"Why don't you take a tea break, Queenie? I want to talk to someone in the hotel business."

Queenie looked hard at the desk clerk for a moment, then came to a decision. "Lily, call Digger, will you. Tell him Madam wishes a private word with him." That said, Queenie turned her attention to the tourists, shepherding them with her outstretched arms back to their cocktails. "That's all, ladies and gentlemen. Show's over."

Lily lifted the phone. Behind me the elevator's metal doors opened, then closed, like a yawn.

# Chapter Four
## Digger, Digger, down under gold digger

Friday, March 31

7:11 p.m.

The plastic plate on the half-open door read MANAGER, GENERAL.

"Knock, knock," I called.

From beyond the door, a Down-Under voice grunted something that sounded like, "Go away."

When in doubt, press ahead. I stepped inside. Right away the office struck me as too small for its furniture. The executive desk, high-back chair, IBM computer and Sony TV console took up three quarters of the room, and an upside down Quantas poster covered most of the far wall. Glancing around, I took in the stack of files leaning like a drunk in the spare corner and the hockey game flickering on the TV screen. I sniffed the air. The room smelled of sawdust, lemon oil and Brut, the aftershave of the lone occupant.

Lone occupant also gave the impression of being somewhat out of place. Lolling ostentatiously in the fake leather chair, with his silver-toed cowboy boots up on the desk and his head cradled in his hands, he looked like the Marlboro Man--with glasses by Coca-Cola. His look--faded blue jeans, red plaid shirt, studio tan, salon-grey curls and dimpled cheeks--was just too good to be true. Except for the heavy wire-frame glasses bridging his nose, he was the image of a cowboy actor in an advertisement for something dangerous.

He was hot, the glasses were not. Behind the spectacles, which weighed heavily on his nose, his eyes floated like specimens in a lab jar--a distant early warning that their owner might have a shortsighted view of the world.

After waiting a full minute for Lone Occupant to acknowledge my presence, during which time he refused to even look my way, I stepped in front of the TV, blocking his view of the hockey game.

"Well, look who's here," he drawled.  Picking up the remote control, he muted the TV.  He made no effort to get up, nor did he offer me a seat.  The room had too little space for a second chair, and clearly the Occupant wasn't about to vacate the one behind the desk.  "It's Comrade Colwell.  Wait 'til I tell the boys down at the Chamber of Commerce."

At first, I was a bit taken aback that this guy would recognize the unknown politician.  Then I realized that Lily or Queenie must have given him a heads up.

I extended my hand, but he merely blinked at it.  "Pleased to meet you, Mister . . .?"

"Digger.  Digger Greenwood."  He cracked his knuckles, then remarried his hands behind his head.  "Don't have much time for politicians myself.  God awful parasites mostly.  Women politicians are even worse, nothing but whiners and bitchers for the most part.  Though I did fancy that Maggie Thatcher.  The world could use a few more like her." He gave me a showy wink.

"Maggie Thatcher and her clones?  Sounds like a great name for a grunge band," I replied with my winningest smile.

"And I loved Ronald Reagan.  Naturally."

"Naturally."  I watched Greenwood's eyes through the Coke-bottle lenses.   This one, I would bet, knew the price of everything.  Now, he was busy figuring out how to play me.

With the heel of his hand, he shunted the magnifying glasses up onto the peak of his nose.  "Back in Australia, they had a saying: If a man had two sons, he'd send one off to become a preacher or a teacher, and he'd keep the smart one at home to run the farm.  Nowadays, I bet the old man would invest good money to make the dumb one a bloody politician."

I didn't miss a beat. "Like Ronald Reagan."

"Ha! You got me there didn't you, darling. Well, I tell you, ol' Ron sure showed all those bureaucratic geniuses down in Washington..."

Interrupting him, I waved my hand in his face. "Excuse me, Mr. Greenback."

"Greenwood." He performed a little scissor kick with his legs and turned his attention back towards the game on TV.

"Greenwood, sorry. This is really interesting and I'd love to hear all about the outback but I'm not here looking for your vote. You seem to have your mind made up there, anyway. Although, as an Australian, you're probably not be eligible to vote."

"Don't you worry, Regina. I can fix that soon enough."

"That's great, Mr. Greenwood, but all I want is a room for the night. I've had a long day and I'd like to put *my*feet up."

He stretched and cracked his knuckles again. "My old gal at the front counter says you're not even packing a credit card. No Visa, no Master Card, and you left home without your American Express. Or won't the capitalist piggies give the comrade any credit?"

"My credit rating is incredible, thank you. I just prefer to pay cash. Keeps things nice and anonymous. You know, no telemarketers."

The man stroked his jaw lovingly, like a Madison Avenue wrangler after a close shave. "In this business you've got to be careful about cash." He affected a cowboy drawl. "Money just ain't what it used to be. Also, a woman alone. It doesn't look good. No reservation, no luggage and no credit card. Very suspicious. Very. We have rules about this kind of thing. We must. You know about rules, don't you? Of course, you do."

Greenwood seemed to be having a ball, but not me. I didn't like his game--especially with a man like him at bat--and I didn't even know what it was called.

"Why don't you go home?" he asked bluntly.

Take a deep breath, Regina. Now, be cool. "Have you noticed the blizzard outside, Mr. Greenwood? And, in case you haven't heard, the mayor has locked out the bus drivers. One could wait hours for a taxi. And, frankly, my dear, I'd rather be watching television."

Greenwood slapped the flat of his hand on the tabletop and snarled. "Bloody unions!" He stared the game on TV for a moment before opening his mouth again. "Have you considered hitchhiking?" he asked. "Some desperate old masher is bound to pick you up."

I forced a smile. "You're not serious, man. Even carjackers will be home with the Oilers on a night like this. Besides, what do you care about my travel plans?" I peered at my reflection in the man's goggles. "I thank you for your interest in my schedule, but it is none of your business."

"Ah, but you're wrong about that. It's my business, darling, and that gives me the right to decide who kips in the hotel."

"Absolute power, eh?"

"Absolutely." He peered at the stacks of documents in the corner. "Somewhere around here we have a sign that says the hotel bloody well reserves the right to refuse service to anyone, or words to that effect."

I looked at the Quantas poster. "Somehow, I'm not surprised."

Greenwood shrugged. "That's the freedom of the marketplace. I have the right to sell what I like to whatever mob I like for whatever price the market will bear."

"Not in this province you don't."

The manager's eyes narrowed. "No? Who says?"

"The law."

"What bloody law?"

"For a start, the *Consumer Protection Act* says you can only rent hotel rooms at publicly posted prices. Then, the *Human Rights Act* you cannot refuse accommodation to anyone without reasonable grounds."

Greenwood swiped the air in front of his nose. "Jesus H. Christ. Don't tell me. Two more stupid statutes to add to the heap. Goddamned do-gooders mucking up the marketplace. Not one of you interfering bastards would last a minute in the real world."

He sounded like he'd made this speech before, and, for a mad moment, I wondered if he fancied offering himself for public office. Printing my sweaty palms in the waxy polish on his desktop, I stared him down. "There's more to the real world than your imaginary marketplace, Mr. Greenwood."

"Like what?"

"Oh, I don't know." I gave him a big Jimmy Carter grin. "Questions of privilege, a prairie sunset, Bif Naked: the world is full of weird and wonderful shit. What's so real about the so-called free market, anyway? It doesn't exist anywhere on this planet, and never did."

Greenwood just looked right through me.

I shrugged and started for the door.

He guffawed like a late-show rustler, then Greenwood drawled, "Now hold your horses a second and listen."

With my hand on the doorknob, I paused, then turned slowly on the balls of my feet. "I have been listening, Mr. Greenwood, and very carefully. Possibly, you are captured by the delusion that I am your standard, government-issue pinko punker. Please also consider that I'm a customer with cash in hand--one of those people who is supposedly always right. I really loved your Crocodile Dundee Does the Chamber Luncheon impersonation and I am heartened to meet a citizen so interested in civic affairs. Someday, I'd really enjoy debating some of the big issues with you but now is not the time. All I want is a room of my own, and--if at all possible--I'd like it today."

Greenwood peeled off his glasses and blew dust off the lenses.

I drummed perspiring fingers on Greenwood's desktop. "Or you can give me your reason why not. In writing."

Greenwood returned his glasses to his nose and flicked some sawdust off the cuffs of his jeans. "Crocodile Dundee? I'm crushed! You really know how to hurt a fella."

I planted the palms of my hands on the top of his desk. "You don't want to give me a room, do you?"

Greenwood struck a new pose, the Thinker, chin in hand. "Nope."

I exhaled slowly. "Why not?"

He folded his arms across his chest and grinned like a TV game show host. "Because."

"Tell me: Would you refuse a room to Oprah?

"Oh, right. So, now I'm a bloody racist as well as a sexist pig? Is that it? Typical." He glared at me over the tops of his glasses.

"What are you then, Mr. Greenwood? A misogynist? Or are you simply having a bad day? Like me."

Greenwood swung his legs off the desk and stood up. "Hey, little lady, there's no need to get nasty. I'm just chatting you up a bit. That's all."

I felt my spine stiffening, but kept my cool. I peeled my hands off the waxy build up on the desktop and stared down at the moist imprint my palms had left on the veneer. Seeing a pad of lined paper sitting at the peak of the leaning stack of files, I reach over, picked it up and put it in front of the hotel manager. I took up a ball-point pen from the desk and uncapped it. With all the formality I could summon, I placed the pen down on the pad with the nib pointing my way. Then I stepped back from the desk and waited.

Greenwood's eyes tracked across the ceiling, then settled on an instant replay on the TV screen. Then it came to me. What an idiot you are, Regina. He was playing hard to get. He wanted me to submit to his power. He want me to flirt, to flatter to him, to be feminine. How gross! But what the hell.

Exasperated, I picked up the hem of Woolly One with the tips of my fingers and curtsied. "Please, sir, may I have room?" I said in a little-girl voice. "Make room in the inn for me, please, sir." I smiled, cute-like. "Or I'll haul your butt before the Human Rights Commission."

He blinked at me and levered himself to his feet. "Let me get this straight: You're not going to leave my private office until I give you a room for the night, or a note explaining my reasons for refusing to do so. Is that it?"

Shoving my hands into my leather pockets, I grinned. "Right. Now we're communicating. Though I must admit that I now want a room mainly because you don't want to give me one!"

A smile grew on Greenwood's face, then he threw up his hands in mock defeat. "All right, okay, you win. I'll get you a room. For one night only. Okay? Too much bloody trouble to type a letter at this time of night. Follow me." He stepped up on his chair, onto his desk blotter, then bounced down to the floor. Flicking off the light switch by the door, he strode out, leaving me alone and in the dark room with the flickering Sony.

In the second before Greenwood turned out the light, I spotted something very strange taped to the back of his office door. On a provincial electoral office map of the city's political constituencies, Greenwood had drawn a magic marker overlay of jagged red lines, like fresh scars on the body politic. That's curious, I thought, before following Greenwood out and around the corner to the front desk.

The carpenters had left, but not their leavings. A pile of wood scraps had been shovelled into a corner and covered with sheets of transparent plastic, like those draped over the lobby furniture. Greenwood placed his hands on the plastic sheeting and vaulted like a gymnast over the counter as the desk clerk scurried out of the manager's way. He studied the room register, flipping through the index with his fingertips. "Here, a hundred-dollar suite, but I'll give you the government rate" He affected a maniacal grin. "Two hundred bucks."

I took a deep breath but said nothing.

Greenwood gave me a crooked grin. "Just kidding. It will cost you sixty. But it's just for tonight. No guarantees for tomorrow. Right?"

"I guess so." I counted out three twenties.

He handed me a key. "There you are then: suite number 701. Hey, what do you know? A prime number! Great!"

Baffled, I stared at the man. He was acting as if he'd just won the lottery. "A prime number? So what?"

He flashed me another grin. "I love prime numbers. Prime numbers are perfect mysteries. Each one is indivisible except by one and itself. "

"I recently met someone like that." I stowed the precious key in my jacket pocket before he could ask for it back.

Greenwood cocked his head but otherwise did not respond. When he wasn't being a jerk, he was a fine figure of a manager. Why, at long last, had he become so accommodating? Perhaps he was one of those people who don't want to put anything in writing. Surely, he had nothing to fear from that notoriously ineffectual body, the provincial Human Rights Commission. Whatever. At least I had a room for the night, a prime room too.

Lily slid a blotting pad onto the plastic-covered counter, then placed a form on top of the blotter. I filled in the blanks. In the "next of kin" slot, I wrote my father's name and phone number. Greenwood hovered nearby, watching me meet his bureaucratic expectations.

"Do I make you nervous, Mr. Greenwood?"

He stepped back and laughed, nervously.

"You can call me, Digger. Everyone does."

"Not quite everyone. What kind of work did you do back in Tasmania?"

"Tasmania?" Greenwood gave me a pained look. "Queensland."

I smiled. "All right, Queensland."

"A bit of this and a bit of that."

"After you left the farm, did you go to college, modelling school, or what?"

"I articled in accountancy," he said, quickly.

"A chartered accountant! I'd never have guessed."

Greenwood blew specks of sawdust off the counter sheet. "No?"

"Tell me, Mr. Greenwood, what gives with your bouncer?"

"Queenie?"

"Yes, Queenie. I made one little joke and she manhandled me like a disorderly drunk."

"She's very good at what she does."

"It's what she does that I'm wondering about."

"She's my assistant. In a bigger place, she'd be in charge of security. Sure, she's a bit too butch but she dresses and speaks beautifully."

"Your guests will be impressed."

"No complaints so far."

"Except mine."

"Right. And you can leave right now, if you want."

I laughed. "Mr. Greenwood, you must be the rudest hotel manager in the city. How, I wonder, do you plan to get anyone to come back to here for a repeat visit? And how on earth do you manage to hang onto your job?"

Lily turned her head to hide a smile.

"Is he like this with everybody?" I asked the desk clerk but she looked away.

Greenwood chuckled, pushed his eyeglasses up his nose, and jumped back over the counter. Landing on his feet, he brushed wood chips off his hands, then pointed a finger at me. "I thought your type didn't care about the bourgeois niceties."

"My type strives for something like a Society of Friends. We've obviously got a way to go."

Greenwood smiled a crooked smile. "Play your cards right, and we can be friends."

Nodding, I put down the pen. "Mates, right?"

"Right." Greenwood shoved his hands into his back pockets.

"What about Norman Water? Was he your mate?"

Greenwood stole a sidelong glance at Lily, then lowered his eyes. "The Water boy? I don't want to talk about him."

"Why not?"

He rocked gently from heel to toe as if to gather momentum for another great leap forward. "Norman was a washout."

"Tell me about him." All ears, I propped my elbows on the counter. "I'd love to hear the whole story."

"Nah."

I waved my room key. "Now that I have a place to stay, there's time for a chat."

"No."

"Yes."

"If you must know, Norman turned up here one day, dripping wet, and wanted me to give him a room. Queenie had kicked him out of the pool upstairs. She told the boy the swimming pool was for residents only. There used to be a sign up there, I think."

"Yet you gave him a room? Without any aggravation?"

Greenwood grinned, sheepishly. "I should never have let him in here, but I'll be buggered if the boy didn't have a brand new credit card tucked in his Speedo. Never been used, not even signed. Said it came in the mail just before his parents packed up. Said he'd been staying with friends. I wasn't too sure about any of that, but we had a spare apartment and he appeared to have some money, so we gave him an apartment. When he ran out of money, we helped him out by giving him a job as well. But what can I say? It didn't work out."

"Now he's dead. End of story, eh?" I studied Greenwood's face.

He looked directly back at me, the eyes narrowing behind his glasses. "That was my fault, was it, Regina?"

I waited for him to continue, but he added nothing. An awkward silence followed.

"What happened to his parents?" I asked at last.

"His dad is with some mutual fund brokerage. He got transferred back east, somewhere near Toronto. He didn't say; I didn't ask. He was a quiet lad. Bit of a drip, if you want the truth of it."

I dropped, for now, the subject of Norman's family. "He had an apartment, I have a room. What's the difference?"

"Nothing much. Physically, they're the same, but the rooms we rent by the day and the apartments we let by the month. At least, we did."

"You did? What if I wanted to rent an apartment now?"

"You're too late--unless you are on staff." Greenwood unhooked the glasses from his ears and polished the lenses on his shirtsleeve. "Norman was the last long-term tenant. Done right, there's a lot more money in hotel rooms than apartments. It's what the market calls progress."

 "And if one day you begin to rent them by the hour, will that be progress, too?"  I started to back away.

Greenwood followed.  "Whatever the market dictates, Regina."

"Colwell.  You can call me Ms. Colwell.  That's what this market dictates," I tapped my chest and backed onto the elevator.

Greenwood held the door open.  "Sure, Regina.  But, if I remember rightly, in the election, you won a pretty narrow majority in this seat.  You'd think a smart lady politician would be a little sweeter to her customers."

"You mean constituents."

"Right." He turned his back on me.

The elevator doors enclosed me inside the elevator, and I floated up to seven.

# Chapter Five
## Bud keeps on budding in

Friday, March 31

7:47 p.m.

The room looked as if it had lost the final round with its last tenant. The bed sheets lay wrinkled and defeated on the floor. The tenant had thrown towels in the bathtub, on the bed, over the television and onto an overturned lamp. An ashtray was overflowing with cigarette butts and the toilet bowel was full of turds.

I decisively flushed the toilet, then went to the bedside table where the phone sat. I righted the reading lamp with a bulb-blistered shade, but it wouldn't work until I screwed the bulb tight in the socket. No big deal. Picking up the phone, I called the front desk. "Lily, Regina Colwell in Room 701. Could you send someone up to make up my room? It looks like the last tenant had a fight with the furniture."

That done, I dialled my home number.

The voice at the other end shouted a cheery hello. It pissed me off that my unwelcome house guest had answered on the first ring.

"Moss, Regina. You sound quite at home. Any messages?"

"Regina who? Do I know you? Say, are you that radical chick with the sexy lips and the great white teeth?"

"Do you mean 'chic' or 'chick'?"

"Okay, chic chick."

"Say, why do print reporters always describe women in physical terms, the feminist nag asked for the umpteenth time?"

"Say what?  Do I hear a sweeping generalization?"

"Moss the bearded reporter, or is it Moss the hairy squatter?"

Moss groaned, and I took a deep, forgiving breath--a strategic pause in the conversation that allowed my house guest to start over.

"Moss the apprentice househusband.  And since you locked your answering machine in the bedroom, I know zip about any messages," he added.

"Sorry, honeybuns, but I'm going to have to lay you off.  If you can't cut it, you'll have to hit the road.  You know about trainees: last hired, first fired."

"Man, you never gave me a chance."

"Quit your whimpering.  Did you feed Tom, my other stray?"

"Yeah, yeah.  That cat wolfs down his food like a dog.  Just hungry for love, I guess.  Like me."

"Gee, Moss, are you and the cat sublimating?"

"Right on, Doc.  You'll have me on the couch next."

"I already have you on my couch, Moss."

"Ha, ha.  Where are you, anyway?  You on your way home?"

"Not yet.  I'm at The Apartment Hotel on Second Avenue, down by the old Helsinki Curling Club."

"So, what's happening down there?  What are you doing?  Throwing rocks at Tories?"

Lying back on the bed, I closed my eyes.  "Seeing a body." I waited for his ears to prick up.

"You're seeing somebody?  Who is it?  Is he bigger than me?"

"Moss, Moss, don't you hacks ever get your facts straight?  I said I saw a body."

"Come on back to your place, and you can see mine."

"A dead body, this was. And one body a day is enough for me, thanks."

"A corpse? Yuck. Was it someone we know? Was that why you rushed off today?"

"Right." I opened my eyes and propped myself up against the headboard. "You know Dr. Corbeau, the coroner? Well, he wanted to find out if I recognized a kid who died in one of the rooms over here. I'm pretty sure I don't, but evidently the boy knew me. At least, he knew my name and number."

"A secret admirer? Read all about it: 'Love-Sick Teen Pines for Pol.'"

"Somehow I doubt it. My guess is that he needed help in some way."

"Hmm. Was it suicide? Like, did he leave a note?"

"They don't seem to know how he died, yet. It could have been anything from AIDS to asthma. The only clue was my name and number."

"Groovy. So are you coming home soon? You can tell me all about it. I'm making poached eggs on toast. It's all I could find in your fridge."

"I'm not that hungry, Moss. Besides, I'm planning on staying here for the night."

"How come? You can't beat my eggs, man. I'm a world-class poacher."

"You've certainly been poaching on *my* turf. No, I'm going to take some time to think."

"When you're done meditating, can I come down and worship at your feet?"

"No, Moss, you cannot. I wore the Doc Martens today."

"For a drink, then? We need to talk about us."

I pushed stray hair away from my face, preparing to make a "for the record" statement. "Moss, there is no 'us.' We need to talk about your departure date. When Robyn showed you the door, you promised to look for your own place right away. You said you were only going to stay on my couch for a day or two. Now, three weeks later, Robyn thinks you're boinking me."

"But we're getting closer, aren't we? Intimacy is coming. Deep down inside, don't you feel it? Soon, I'll know all your secrets, Regina."

"You want to know a secret, Moss? I like you fine, but right now, deep down inside, I really, really resent your abuse of my hospitality."

"Gosh, Regina, you vote-chasers sure do beat around the bush. Why don't you say what you mean? Get to the point, eh?"

"Moss!"

"Look, let's not argue on the phone. Let's do it face to face. I'll meet you down there? Just for a drink. I won't stay long, and I promise to go quietly when it's time."

"Forget it, Moss. I know about reporters. They're always plying legislators with liquor, trying to dig up...."

"Buried bodies?"

"...dirt."

A loud knocking at the door interrupted the conversation.

"I've got to go, Moss, really."

"One drink?"

The knocking stopped. I heard a key in my lock. "Okay, okay." For a second, I considered asking Moss to bring me a change of clothes. But when I thought about him going through the private things in my bedroom, I quickly rejected the idea.

"I'll get there around ten." Moss hung up.

The door opened, and a man pulling a mop and a pail backed rudely into the room. His sweat pants hung low on his flanks, exposing too much of his buttocks. His rear pocket bulged heavily with the weight of a Sony Walkman, and a twisted black wire connecting his butt to the headphones noosed around his neck. His sagging T-shirt and down-at-the-heels hightops were designed for bony adolescents, but under the sweats the guy packed the wintry flab of a middle-aged man.

"Later," I heard Moss say as I dropped the receiver on the bed and yelled at the intruder, "Hey! What are you doing in here?"

"Toilet overflowing," the man announced. "People tripping out downstairs."

As he turned I saw, with alarm, that I knew the guy. The square head, the crew cut and the hooded eyes belonged to that relentless consumer of my legislative services, Mr. Bud Budinski.

A mentally challenged man, Bud had been waiting for me at the campaign headquarters the morning after my late-night squeaker of an election victory. I hadn't even been sworn in yet, but Bud gave me hell for being late for work, and that day I helped him with his unemployment-insurance claim. Within hours, he'd reappeared with a complaint against his landlord. In the weeks following, he marched a parade of difficulties to my attention: a bus-pass hassle, a utility-bill dispute and several learner's permit problems. Now a regular visitor to my storefront office, Bud was, by far, the single most demanding of all my constituents. At times, I felt like his personal social worker.

"Bud!" I exclaimed, with all the professional enthusiasm I could muster.

"Hi, Regina!" Bud's face split into a wide grin. "Wicked!"

I touched his elbow. "You first. What are you doing here?"

"Got a job." He stuck out his chest. "Hotel handyman. Cool, huh?"

"Hey, that's great, Bud. When did you start?" Steering him into the bathroom, I tiptoed through the flood, rattled the toilet handle, then made way for my constituent.

Gingerly, Bud picked up the sodden towels, looked around for a place to put them, then dumped them into the bathtub. He took up his mop and started to slosh water around the bathroom floor.

"Been on the job three months now." Bud's face was aglow. "It's called E.T.P, the Employment Training Program."

Bud laboured over his words, sounding out each syllable and punctuating each sentence with a downward chop of his chin. "The government pays the hotel, and they pay me to work for them. Heather, your Heather, signed me up." Just saying Heather's name brought light to his eyes. "You remember me always cruising in to see you guys." Bud paused for breath, leaning on his mop like a pro.

"That's right. We haven't seen you around for weeks."

"A job keeps a body busy."

"How long is the program? When do you finish the course, I mean?"

Bud frowned. "Huh?"

"How long does the training last?"

His eyes brightened with understanding. "Got three months to go. But they might hire me full time afterwards. And, get this, if I get on full time, the hotel might even give me a room on the staff floor where Greenwood and Queenie and Herb stay."

"That's great." I said without believing it.

Bud defiantly pushed the mop across the wet floor. "The doctors call me subnormal, but Bud can still work."

"That's right, Bud."

"Don't get much money, Regina. The chambermaids do the same work as me, but they get paid a lot more." He looked up suddenly; Bud had an idea. I almost saw the light bulb blazing over his head.

"Can you help me get more pay? Can you tell those dudes to give me more money?"

I pursed my lips, something I do when thinking about money. "Guess I can try, Bud. Did Greenwood hire you?"

"Yeah." Bud swabbed the floor right and left. "He's nice, that man, a truly awesome dude."

"Is he really?" I watched Bud slop the puddle around the floor, the tide rising against the skirting of one wall then turning to splash against the other. "Did you know Norman Water?"

Letting the mop slide to a stop, Bud bowed his head. "He passed away."

"Yes, I know he died. Was he nice, too?"

Bud's chin chopped the air. "Oh, yeah. Used to let me watch TV in his room. And really wicked videos. He was nice, a really awesome dude."

"TV?" I tried to imagine the scene. Norman Water and Bud Budinski in front of a TV set, learning Hollywood slang from "adult action" movies.

"We played Nintendo, watched TV and videos. Until they took it away."

"Took what away? The TV?" I pictured faceless men walking off with the TV set. "Who took it away, Bud?"

"Queenie said he hadn't paid for it."

"Queenie? Queenie De Lis?"

With a twist of the mop handle, Bud mumbled "Yeah."

"What happened to Norman's furniture?"

"It got wet." Using both hands, Bud ploughed the mop into the puddle.

I glanced around the apartment, then back at bathroom floor. "Wet? How did the furniture get wet, Bud?"

Bud screwed up his face. "Don't know." He took a break from mopping, and the flood leaked out of the bathroom onto the bedroom carpet. "Will you help me, Regina? We're talking major money here. Big time. Got rent to pay, things to do."

"I told you, Bud, I'll try." For no reason that I could see, the precarious hold of the sweat pants on Bud's waist captured my attention. Then the image morphed into an idea. "What about Norman's clothes, Bud? I've just realized he had none in his room."

"Went to the cleaners, maybe. Hotel sends them out."

"To the cleaners, eh?"

I'd have to think about that. Then just as I stooped to help Bud squeeze the mop, the door flew open and a chambermaid charged into the room with a toilet plunger in her fist.

The maid had furious eyes and a jagged crew cut. She wore a silver ring in her nose, Cinderella-sized army boots, a jaundiced smock and greying jeans. The smock and jeans were stretched like tourniquets around her stomach and crotch. With her high cheekbones, eagle nose and copper skin she had to be Amerindian.

The young woman pushed roughly by. Plunging her tool into the toilet bowl, she attacked it madly until the bowl drained with a loud sucking sound. Stepping back, the maid tossed the plunger out into the hall. Only then did she acknowledge my existence and, remembering her manners, she reached back to thump on the door with the heel of her fist. "You want your bed turned down?" she snarled.

I started to say that I wanted my bed changed but before I could get it out, the maid turned on Bud. Without any obvious provocation, she leaned over and grabbed the mop out of his hand. "Give me that, you moron! You make more effing mess than you clean up."

The maid glowered at me, until I withdrew to a neutral corner of the bedroom. As soon as I moved, the maid began, in hushed tones, to abuse her fellow worker. "Always have to clean up other people shit. Work like dog, and nobody gives a shit. Buddy, you dumb bastard, why don't you get out of here? Go on. Get lost!"

"Doing my best, Rose," Bud whined plaintively.

"Doing my best, Rose," the woman mimicked the whine, mercilessly mocking the hapless Bud. "Look what you done, you stupid creep. Get out of here." Although Bud had already backed out of the bathroom, Rose took a stab at Bud's gut with the mop handle. "Git!"

Enough, already. I stepped in. "Chill, woman. Take it easy. He's not going to take your damn job."

Rose let the mop fall, folded her arms under her breasts and gave me a black look. "Not your business." War had been declared.

I held my ground. "It's my room," I said and instantly regretted it.

We held each other's stares for a moment, then Rose stepped aside. "Your room, you clean it," she shot back.

"Okay, give me some fresh sheets." I opened the door to let them both out.

Bud bowed his head and shuffled off, but Rose did not leave. Instead, before I could grab it, she picked up the mop and started attacking the mess on the bathroom floor. "Stupid asshole! Piss all over floor. Shit and piss. Sure, leave me wiping up the goddamn piss and shit." She wrung the mop's neck, then slapped it back on the floor, making a huge racket.

The violent mopping action had raised Rose's sleeves, exposing on her left forearm an elaborate tattoo of a red rose and blue thorns.

The tattoo was the most ornate and exquisite tattoo artistry I'd ever seen. Fascinated, I leaned forward for a closer look. Rose responded by turning away.

Ever the peacemaker, I decided to lend Rose a hand. Taking the one remaining bath towel off the rack, I got down on my knees to mop up the water that had leaked onto the bedroom carpet. Not until the task was complete, did Rose file her complaint. "Hey, what you doing? That not your job. That my job!"

Perfect timing, I thought, and tried to make a joke of it. Waving my hand above my head, I called out, "Shop steward!"

Rose stared down at me, her eyes hard and unforgiving.

I stood up, rinsed my hands in tap water and returned Rose's stare, but with my eyebrows raised expectantly. Rose's work had caused her uniform smock to ride up her torso. The outfit looked so painfully tight around the housekeeper's breasts and stomach that I couldn't help wondering if the hotel or the employee had chosen the garment.

"What's that?" Rose screwed up her face. "Shop stew-ward."

"Shop steward? Someone from the union." I climbed to my feet. "They handle grievances."

"Union. We got no goddamn union here." Rose started to say something more, paused for a second, then spat it out. "What good they do anyway? They just take your money for nothing."

"Working people should stick together. That's what a union is."

"One of them union bosses came round one time. Big fat white man, in a shiny car."

"There are some good unions, hard working, democratic organizations."

"Sure. Some fat white man sit in some comfy office, smoke cigar."

"They're not all like that. I could introduce you..."

"Shit, no!" Rose slam-dunked the mop into the pail.

Try as I might, I couldn't keep my eyes off the young woman. Her hair seemed to have been cropped with a machete--possibly as some kind of protest against professional hairdressing, which really appealed to me. I couldn't help wondering if Rose had done it herself, or if she had paid hard-earned money to have it barbered that way. "If you don't mind my asking, what do you get paid?"

The housekeeper gave me another stony look. "You looking for a job?"

I smiled. "Not exactly."

Rose toyed with the hem of her uniform. "Minimum wage plus twenty-five cents. Plus tip. If you get any."

"You get good tips?"

"What do you care? You with the hundred-dollar shoes," she added under her breath.

"What?" I pretended that I hadn't heard.

With her little Cinderella boot propping the door open, Rose drove the pail out into the hall.

"Mind if I call you Rose?" I asked.

With her foot still holding the door, Rose looked over her shoulder. "Don't call me, I call you." A smile broke on her face, then faded fast. Briefly, before becoming tight-lipped again, she had exposed a row of tangled, yellow teeth.

"You want your bed fix or what?" Rose demanded. The way she said it made it sound more like a threat than a question.

Stealing another glance at the thorny stem on the rose tattoo, I reconciled myself to the fact that Rose had little time for nice chats.

"Sure, and I'll need some more towels." I offered up the sopping bundles from the tub and the floor. The maid snatched the bundle out of her hands, jammed the door open again and hurled the towels out into the hall.

Returning once more, Rose nudged me out of the way. "Got lotsa shit to do." She whipped the sheets off the bed and fitted their replacements in seconds. She whipped the drapes across the windows, rammed a chair against the wall and yanked down the bedspread. The cleanup amounted to a direct assault on the objects the hotel paid Rose to protect. I had my own private demonstration of the Greenwood School of Hospitality and Rose's individual style of heavy-metal housekeeping.

I waited helplessly at the door while the housekeeper angrily finished her repetitive tasks. Part of me was dying to interrupt and to offer to share these chores, but in the end all I could say was a whispered, "Thanks."

Rose inspected her work, then quickly checked her own appearance in the bathroom mirror. From the way she posed, twisting around to view her reflected bottom, I guessed that the jeans at least were probably the employee's choice.

"Are you Native?" I asked, trying not to stare.

Rose stared back, an ocean away from Discovery. "Native?"

"Indian."

"Who wants to know?" Her dark eyes bored through mine.

I raised my hands apologetically. "I just wondered."

"I'm half," Rose said, her lips hardly moving.

"Half?"

"Half Indian, half white man."

"Which Nation are you from?"

Her brow furrowed. "Canada."

"No, I mean which First Nation?" I asked with an apologetic laugh.

"First Nation?" Rose looked blank.

"Tribe. Which tribe? What band?" My palms began sweating, and I joined my hands, praying for peace. And understanding.

Rose stuck out her chin. "You sure ask question."

"I'm sorry. I was just interested in where you come from."

"Here."

"Oh."

The conversation was hard going. On the hustings, I'd had learned the canvasser's rule not to waste precious minutes on the Hostiles. But I still felt the new politician's urge to connect, the liberal's guilty need to relate, especially with persons of colour. How could I aspire to a career of public service if I failed this simple test? The prospect of humiliating defeat drove me to try one last push. The direct approach. "Did you know Norman Water?"

Fingering the ring in her nose, Rose said, "Who wants to know?"

I bowed my head, modestly. "I do."

Rose looked at the floor. "He your friend?"

"No," I said quietly.

Rose's jaw muscles clenched and her eyes darkened. "That goddamn Popsicle deserved to die!" Then she retreated from the room, slamming the door behind her.

I watched her go, then stood for a minute staring at the door. All right, Rose hated Norman but what on earth could he have done that was so bad she wanted him dead?

I kicked off my hundred-dollar brand name shoes, threw the leather jacket on the bed and explored the "suite." It had the usual frequent-flyer equipment: bed, bathroom, bureau, cheap print of a bad painting and "adult action" movies on the pay TV. The kitchenette in one corner was a remnant of the room's previous life as an apartment. On the bedside table a display card promoting the Rooftop Garden swimming pool crowded a clock radio, a telephone and the lamp with the bulb-blistered shade.

My tired eyes transformed the snow-white walls, the earth-brown carpet, the summer-blue ceiling, the forest-green nylon bedspread and the pine-coloured crushed velvet drapes from banal interior decoration into a work of art, a neat abstract impression of the Canadian landscape. Perfectly impersonal, so completely anonymous, the room could be anywhere.

After a hard day trying not to get screwed by Tories, reporters and accountants, I wanted nothing more than to veg  in the company of servile machines inside a safe, clean, numbered space. That was the idea anyway.

# Chapter Six
## Is a bad dad is better than a mad mom?

Friday, March 31

9:48 p.m.

I touch-toned the male parent's number, my fingers walking the steps from digital memory.  As usual Dad wanted to know exactly where I was and what I was doing.  As usual, I did not tell him the whole truth.  I told him I was at the hotel for some meetings and left it at that.  Why try to explain my reasons for staying in the hotel?  I could barely explain them to myself--so I deliberately did not tell Dad about my day.

Anyhow, I knew that, whatever the circumstances, my sire would never approve of his one and only daughter going away without a toilet kit or a change of underwear.  A widower of twenty years, he stubbornly stuck to his teaching post, keeping home and garden, resisting all my urgings to get him retired out to the West Coast.  We chatted about safe topics--his greenhouse, his cardiologist, his Grade 12 English class--before I asked my question.

"I wonder if, by any chance, you had this kid in one of your classes.  Chances are that he didn't go to John A. MacDonald, but I thought I'd ask."

"I can't remember them all, you know. I've had thousands of students in my day."

"Did you ever teach a kid named Norman Water?  He may have been a competitive swimmer."

"Why, yes . . . yes, I did.  He was in my Grade 10 English class four years ago.  Sat in the back and never said a word."

"Great.  What else can you tell me about him?"

"I won't remember him at all except that Mrs. Kite said the boy was brilliant.  He got 90 percent in math and never did a stitch of work.  Did the boy mention me to you?"

"No, Dad. He's dead."

"Oh, hell. How?"

"The police found him in a hotel room down here."

"Drugs?"

"They can't say yet."  Handset in hand, I chasséd towards the window and peaked through the drapes at the snow drifting in the street below.  "Can you tell me anything more? What about his parents?"

"I don't think we ever saw either of them at the school."

"Unlike me, eh? Okay, thanks, Dad.  You've been a big help."

I checked the hour on the clock radio and excused myself with a promise of a family dinner at his place, Sunday evening.

Wanting no face-off at my bedroom door, I decided to wait for Moss in the lobby.  On duty still, her blouse starched and her bifocals upright on her nose, Lily stood behind the counter, boxed in up to her shoulders, like a potted plant.

I had stopped by merely to request a seven o'clock wake-up call but, as Lily wrote the message down in a pinched copperplate, I had to ask how she was doing.  "You work long hours," I said.

"They're not too bad.  I've been on afternoons all week.  Tomorrow, I switch to days.  That's only eight hours off before I come to work., it's called 'a short change,' for good reasons," Lily confided in a soft voice.

I leaned closer to hear her better.  "You work weekends, too?"

"Sometimes.  We desk clerks work one weekend on, the next one off.  That way we cover all the shifts, and I don't miss too much on the soaps." Lily smiled with her eyes.

"You've been here a while?"

"Not very long. I came last fall when they started remodelling."

"You like the place?"

Lily's head shrank a centimeter into her frilly shell. "It's a job."

"Where did you work before?"

"For twenty-two years, I filed reports at the provincial soils lab, but they privatized the operation, and the new owner laid off most of us."

"You must have been very upset."

"Not really. I found it pretty tedious there. Most of the time we sat around with nothing to do."

Trying a less controversial topic, I asked, "You live near here?"

"Yes. In fact, I'm a constituent of yours."

"Well, then, I'm very pleased to meet you." I picked up Lily's hand. Her skin felt dry and cold.

"Lily White. I think I even voted for you last time. So, please don't joke about my name."

"Well, thank you, Ms. White."

Wow, I was thinking, the things some parents do to their kids. "Are you an NDP supporter?"

"Please call me, Lily. No, I usually vote for the woman, if there's one on the ballot. Although I dislike the really strident feminists." The smile lines showed around Lily's eyes.

Lowering my voice, I asked, "What's Greenwood like, as a boss?"

Lily quickly scanned the lobby, making sure we were alone. "Oh, he gets things done. He's tough and he's a bit of a nut, but sometimes he makes you laugh. And, without his glasses, he's also quite handsome."

"Yeah? Handsome is as handsome does. He just acted weird around me."

"That's just his Australian Rules; that's what he calls them. He likes to keep people off guard. It helps him stay ahead of the game."

"Fight to the death, eh? Did you know Norman Water?"

"Yes and no. We only worked together for a few weeks."

"What was he like?"

Lily slowly shifted her weight from one foot to the other, then from the other to the one, and back. "I don't like to speak ill of the dead."

Gently, I pressed the point. "You didn't like him?"

"Oh, no. He seemed like a nice boy, always polite but... " Lily quickened her little jig.

"But what?"

"He was rather too fond of playing the fool. A bit of a joker, if you know what I mean?"

"No." I kept perfectly still, trying not to jangle Lily's nerves.

Lily fingered the ruff on her blouse. "Well, one might say that he had quite a peculiar sense of humour."

"How so?"

With her hands flapping, Lily shook off the question.

"All right. Tell me why Rose hates him so much?"

Lily's eyebrows shot up. "Hates him? I don't think so. Oh, no. To my certain knowledge, she was his sweetheart."

"You're kidding!" This was surprising news. Had Lily invented a story for her own private soap opera? It did not make any sense. Less than an hour ago, Rose told me she wanted Norman dead. "Rose and Norman?"

"Yes."

"Forgive me but it's hard to imagine Rose as anyone's sweetheart."

"It's true."

I gestured at the work area behind the counter, and asked, "Were you here when Norman got fired? He did get fired didn't he?"

Lily followed the sweep of my hand. "Mr. Greenwood transferred him."

"How come?"

"Problems, little problems. I don't like to talk about them. That's all in the past now, isn't it?" Lily looked away, her face grim.

I felt a cold breeze around my ankles as the front door opened and Moss made his entrance, brushing the snow off his beard and parka as he came in from the cold. With his ringlets and whiskers, his scuffed Hush Puppies, and the lived-in look of his corduroy suit he looked a bit like my idea of a favourite uncle. He beamed at me, put his arm around my shoulders and gave me a quick proprietary hug.

"Hey man, how are you doing? Be with you in a mo'. I passed a major pileup on the way here and have to call the rag with the tip. Our readers love car crashes. But my cell phone battery is dead. Can you lend me a quarter?"

I fished in my pocket and brought out my wallet, but I had no change, only bank notes. "Lily, let me introduce you to my friend, Moss."

"Your boyfriend?" Lily asked, quickly sizing up the man.

"You are a very perceptive lady," Moss said to Lily.

"No." I was firm. "We are just friends. Right, Moss?"

"Sure, man."

"Lily, can you change a twenty? Moss needs to report an accident."

The clerk laid the bill on top of her cash register, then performed the ritual of money changing. She counted the bills: two fives and a handful of loonies and silver then stopped. She swept the coins back in the till, then started over. Twice, she made mistakes, then corrected them. Obviously flustered, she murmured sincere apologies as she handed over the money, bills for Regina, coin for Moss.

"Grab a table for us. I'll be there in a flash," Moss said.

"What would you like to drink?"

"A brew, please. A cold one."

I stepped into the gloom of the bar. Arguing politics with drunks is a total time-waster so I avoided bars in the district as a rule. But right off I could tell that the Oasis Saloon suffered from a serious personality disorder. The side wall was filled with video-lottery machines. At one end of the room, a silent hockey game flickered across a giant TV screen, at the other end huge speakers pounded out Madonna's "Love Song." The sight and the sound didn't jive at all. Equally disliking both distractions, I compromised and sat midway between the two, at a table beneath a rubbery palm tree.

The next number was a techno number, the kind of music you feel rather than hear, the kind that's made for dancing rather than listening. Somehow the management had forgotten all about the dance floor in their plans, for tables and chairs filled every spare yard of floor space--surely some kind of bylaw infraction. Beer fumes, second-hand smoke and paint fumes uneasily mingled in the windowless room. Even the atmosphere was fighting for air.

Greenwood and Queenie had probably intended to establish a hard-drinking, tough-talking kind of sports bar--somewhere for the guys to gather after a game. Maybe it was just the blizzard but, from what

I could see, the hard-drinking guys and their honky-tonk women had yet to take over the Oasis. Perhaps, the place would do better with the after work crowd.

Once my eyes had adjusted to the gloom, I found myself alone with the server. Thankfully, Queenie had not been at the door to greet me. The server was a handsome, twentyish, red-corseted woman with a blonde flattop.

The corset was unbelievable. It pushed and shoved the server's body in all directions: covering her butt like a diaper, squeezing her waist like a medieval girdle, and shielding her boobs under a warlike bustier. A tag pinned to one of the warheads identified the owner as Fern.

"What'll it be tonight, honey?" Fern asked the palm tree.

"Just a beer and a diet Coke, please. And could you turn down the techno a touch. No one is listening, and it's hard to hear people talk."

"Sure thing, honey. Beer and a diet Coke. What kind of beer, Hon? Does your date have a favourite brand?"

"Any kind. They all taste pretty much the same, don't they?"

"You got me there, you know. Never touch the stuff. How about a German beer?" Fern had a different way of talking. She looked the perfect Nordic type, but her accent sounded like a pale imitation of a black disk jockey from the Deep South. Jive but jarring.

"No. Nothing too expensive. Let's try a local brand."

"Sure thing, Hon," Fern said, without enthusiasm, and strode away managing somehow to roll her hips while keeping her back infantry straight.

I watched Fern's performance as she dropped three ice cubes into a six-ounce glass and then added squirts of Coke, until a thick lick of white foam crept over the rim. The server picked up a pair of cardboard coasters and a tall beer glass. She sashayed over to my little round table, placed the glasses on the coasters then dipped, Bunny-style, to tip the beer into the tall glass.

Just as Fern straightened up, Queenie looked in for a second. Startled, the server knocked over the glass, and I felt a tall glass of cold beer splash into my lap.

Fern ran over to fetch a tea-towel from the bar. In the rush, she completely forgot to sashay. She leaned over, rather than dipping down, to sponge up the mess and her breasts almost tumbled out of their armour. Embarrassed for her, I took over the job. "Let me do it," I implored her..

The server straightened her uniform, checked the doorway for Queenie--who had vanished, and marched off to replace the beer.

I had hardly finished mopping up when Fern came back, plunked down the replacement beer and stuck out a demanding hand. "Mind if I collect for the drinks now, Hon? Going off shift soon, and I'd like to cash out." Fern offered not a hint of an apology.

"No problem." I picked up the bill. Three dollars for a tiny Coke! What am I paying for here? Ice, water, syrup, chemicals and a few bubbles. Water should be free, I silently protested. We already paid for it with our taxes. It's amazing what they'll do to get people to pay for packaging. From previous readings, I knew that the ingredients, listed in the small print on the side of a pop can, sounded pretty gross. Carbonated water, caramel colour, aspartame, phosphoric acid, flavours, citric acid, sodium benzoate and caffeine. Why do I keep on drinking this stuff? I guess I like the taste. Still, I could not forget reading somewhere that you could clean toilet bowls or remove the rust from battery terminals with the stuff.

I flipped over the bill ready to argue my case with the server, then thought, why bother. It had been too long a day for any more hassles. Why blame someone for doing a job?. Pay the bill and no protests! From long habit, I counted the money as I took it out of my wallet. For some reason, there looked to be a few dollars less than there ought to be. I rewound the day's financial transactions in my mind, but could not figure out where the money had gone. I backtracked over the day again then paused in the hotel lobby. Had Lily made a mistake? What about me?

# Chapter Seven
## Water, water everywhere but there is no such thing as a free drink.

Friday, March 31

10:11 p.m.

Moss shucked off his parka and slung it over the back of the chair. Mounting the chair from the rear, he sat for a moment, scratched his beard and stared lovingly at the bubbles in his beer. He put his hands on the table, squared the coaster under the glass with his left hand, then hoisted the beer with his right. After a long swallow, he set down the glass, exhaled happily and wiped the foam off his moustache. "Man, that's good," he said at last. "So tell me about your stiff."

"Stiff? Jesus, Moss. He was a boy--just a kid really--squatting in a fifth-floor apartment." I pointed upstairs. "They found him in his bathtub."

Moss tilted curly head. "What did he look like?"

"Thin, pale, greasy hair. A very ordinary-looking boy, I'd say."

"Ordinary white boy, dead in the water, eh? Know his name?" Moss set down his beer, reached into his pocket and pulled out a notepad.

"Water. Norman Water."

"Water, water." Moss clicked his pen. "Cause of death? Drowning, poisoning, pollution?"

"No idea. It could have been suicide, but it didn't look like it. Hell, what do I know? Maybe he got sick. He sure didn't look as if he'd been eating properly."

"Dieting?"

"Unemployed, more likely. I doubt if he had been working recently. He sure didn't look as if he had any money. His place was empty, not a stick of furniture in sight."

"So, definitely not murdered for his money? I don't like murders anyway. Floods and famine are more my style."

"Murder? Maybe, but I don't know. I saw no bullet holes or knife wounds or anything gory like that. And, get this, he died behind a locked door."

"The classic locked door mystery, eh? Did you spot any drug paraphernalia upstairs?"

"No, but it could have been an overdose, I suppose. The boy died in his bath, but I have a feeling that he didn't drown. The tub had hardly any water in it."

Moss bit the top of his pen. "A body can drown in six inches of water."

"Sure. Or he could have fallen and bumped his head. I just don't have a clue." I sucked at an ice cube. "The really weird thing is that he had my name and number written on his hand."

"Interesting." Moss reached for his glass and took a quick swig of beer. "Home or work?"

"My work number. That's why the coroner called me." I swallowed the rest of the ice cube.

Moss scribbled a note. "Was he a runaway?"

"The opposite. His folks moved away and left him behind."

"Runaway parents, now there's an angle. A sign of the times, eh?"

"I guess." Out of the corner of my eye, I noticed a shadow in the doorway. Turning to check it out, I saw Queenie step across the threshold. I tensed, ready for another duel, but the heavy ignored me and muscled her way past the clutter of tables and chairs towards the bar. Fern handed Queenie a stack of bank notes wrapped in cash-register tape. Queenie fanned the notes, swatted the server on the bottom with the fan, and then began counting the money with a wet finger. Fern watched the count from a safe distance.

I returned my eyes to Moss. "The hotel is a madhouse. Everyone working here acts so squirrelly."

"Cabin fever. It's been a long winter."

"It's got to be more than the weather. It's as if they are all acting out roles in a Monty Python remake."

"Fawlty Towers, Episode Twenty-Two?"

"You should see them. It's like a costume party here. The manager dresses like a cowboy, the handyman trudges around in a track suit, the bouncer over there wears a dinner jacket and they have our server squeezed into a corset designed by a young Hugh Hefner."

Moss gave Fern the eye. "She looks great."

"How would you like to walk around half-naked in that outfit?"

"The cross-dressing bit would probably be a tad too kinky for my rag." Moss rolled up his sleeves and examined his hairy arms. "With the right electrologist, you think I could start a career as a lingerie model?"

"Not likely." I slowly stirred the ice cubes in my drink. "I'd hate having to wear a uniform at work."

"Your Doc Martens and leather jacket are a uniform, Reggie. Well, maybe not a uniform. Let's call it a costume. It's your punk politician costume and it fits how the press gallery has branded you. People like dressing up. Look at your beloved Legislature. The speaker, a chemical engineer, dresses up like an English lawyer and the sergeant-at-arms parades about like a pensioner from the Crimean War. They're masquerading as characters from Dickens. Someone should tell them old Chuck died long before they laid the cornerstone of the Legislative building."

"I don't like being a slave to fashion anymore than I like uniforms. It's hardly fashionable for politicians to wear leather jackets. That's why I like doing it. And of course, the legislature is pure political theatre, except that most of the  political actors wear the same uniform blue or grey suit."

"I thought you'd love uniforms.  Everyone equal, you know?"

"Everyone the same, you mean?  That's not my idea of equality.  For example, in this place I'll bet that only the managers get to choose their own costumes, but even their costumes tell me they'd rather be someplace else.  The legislature is like an antic gentleman's club where they all dress up in suits and play like kindergarten kids.  But this place seems more like an asylum masquerading as the Ritz Carlton."

"What does it matter what people wear, if they do their jobs?"

"My point, exactly.  Uniforms are not certificates of competence, nor are costumes.  Look at the place.  Do you believe these folks qualify as expert hoteliers?  The manager actively aims to displease.  He's also hired, as his assistant, a dandified thuggish woman who packs enough beef to turn cowhands into vegans.  Both of them acted weirdly towards me, and I haven't a clue why.  The manager tried to prevent me getting a room, and the thug tried to toss me out on the street."

"Yea?"  Moss perked up.  "Talk about 'exclusive.'  Wow.  They actually tried to bar you?  Why?"

I shrugged.  "I don't know.  Greenwood, the manager, opposes votes for women, and the bruiser, Queenie, could not tell I was joking about being a sex worker."

"A hooker?  You?"  Moss laughed.  "Forgive me, but that is funny!"

"I also met a housekeeper who hates her job, her life and everything else--and a handyman whose wages come from some federal training program."

"Homo habilis."

"What?"

"The kind where the handyman job disappears when the funds dry up?"

"Right, and that's not all. Everyone has a different line on the deceased. Greenwood, the manager, says he thought of him as a little drip. Rose, the housekeeper, said she was glad he died. The handyman, Bud, described him as 'nice,' but Bud also called Greenwood 'nice,' and I saw no sign of that. Lily, out at the front desk, told me that Water was a joker. It makes you wonder. Eh?"

For a moment, Moss's attention seemed drawn to the bubbles in his beer. "Colourless, odourless, tasteless Norman," he mused. Moss does that sometimes. Sometimes he just drifts off into his own little dream world.

"Like water, water."

"What?"

"The universal solvent." Moss looked me in the eye. "So, Reggie, you've been playing detective? Trying to solve the mystery, eh?"

"Not really. But it sure bothers me that he died with my name on his hand. For the life of me, I cannot figure out how he knew me."

"That's no mystery. You're a public figure; he was a constituent."

"Sure, but who, except someone in big trouble, would have my number inked on the palm of their hand? And why didn't he call?"

"Who knows? Maybe he wanted a passport, or welfare, but felt too tired, or sick, or stoned to get out of the bath and pick up the phone."

"Maybe he *was* in big trouble. And now he's dead." Visualizing the scene with the corpse in the bath, I crossed my arms against the sudden chill creeping over me. "Think about it, Moss. He was just a kid."

"It's sad, sure, but why worry about it?  You didn't snuff him, and you sure can't help him now.  Are the cops on the case?"

Nodding, I took a quick sip of Coke.  "And Corbeau, the coroner."

"Well, then, as soon as the old bird files his report, you'll know how your admirer died.  Chill, Regina.  No need to feel guilty, man."

"I suppose not."  I buffed my palms on Woolly One.

Moss drained his glass and looked around the saloon.  "A skill-testing question: Why did the brains behind the place call it The Apartment Hotel?"

"Poverty of imagination?  Trying to have it both ways?  Who knows?"

"Functionalism sucks," he declared.

"I read that somewhere.  Did you write it?"

"No, but I will.  This room is as ugly as sin.  Man, do I hate what creeping concrete has done to the town.  I actually preferred the ticky-tacky wooden boxes in the old neighbourhoods to the Giant Economy Size boxes they're putting up now.  The Indians lived in cones of deerskin, and the Inuit built domes of snow.  What makes us so ... square, eh?  Even Rotary Park is a rectangle."

"Surely, it's just a matter of money.  Boxes are the cheap way to package stuff, whether it's corn flakes or clerk typists.  It's the bottom line, stupid.  Have I got that right, Mr. President?"

"Americans didn't invent greed.  Don't give them all the credit."

I rattled the ice cubes in my glass. "My Dad used to take me for Sunday walks in Rotary Park."

"You don't want to go there now, man.  It's covered with doggy-doo and take-out trash.  The trees are dying, and the waterfront stinks.  It's a mess."  Moss swilled the dregs of his beer around the bottom of his glass.  "Maybe it's too late to save this dump from itself.  Those in charge don't care, and the rest don't care who's in charge."

Moss drew a line across the page and closed his notebook.

"Do you have any ideas about Norman Water?"

Moss shrugged. "Water never dies. "

"What?"

"It's called the hydrological cycle, man. Moisture from plants and lakes evaporates, gathers in clouds, then falls back to the earth as rain or snow to feed the flowers and trees from whence it came in the first place. Every drop there ever was is still here; it never disappears.

"Is that what you wordsmiths call a diversion? "

"Sure. But it took your mind off the kid for a second, didn't it?"

"Let's get some air, smart ass. The smells in here are really getting to me. I'll probably have a headache in the morning and I'm only swigging Coke." I put on my jacket. "We can do some exploring."

Taking him by the hand, I pulled Moss through the lobby. Lily poked her head up from behind the counter—perhaps to register that the politician was leading the reporter astray, not the other way around. We took the elevator up to the roof.

"Behold the Rooftop Garden."

"I can't see a thing."

"If I could find a light switch, we could look around." After fumbling around in the dark for a minute, I gave up. "Let's just go outside. Follow me closely, and please don't fall in the pool."

We made our way around the pool to a glass door leading to the roof. Pushing against the crash bar and through the door, I zipped up my jacket. The snow was falling more gently now but it still felt chilly outside. Through the snow, the lights of the office towers twinkled in the night.

"It's still snowing a bit."

"Enough snow already. "

"Maybe not. That's our drinking water falling from the sky. Did you know that fresh water amounts to only one percent of all the water in the world? The rest is sea water or polar ice."

"There's been no shortage of wet stuff this winter, Moss."

"But the land around here is drying up."

"Yeah? "

"Every time you pave it over, clear cut trees, drain wetlands... "

"...to put up a parking lot... "

"...water gets diverted from its natural course and heads straight out to sea. Then the water tables drop, the land dries up, trees and creatures die, even people. We only get fresh water from snow and rain and if we wall it off with concrete and asphalt it runs right by us. And the land dries out, which only adds to global warming. "

We stood there on the roof watching the snow and looking at the city below.

"I really like the city lights, especially the ones on the tall buildings."

"I thought you hated the banks."

"With a passion. But I love the lights."

"I hate the bank buildings, those ugly, ugly office towers."

"You're right but I still like the lights. They're beautiful. Look at them twinkling."

"They're the pyramids of our time, vanity architecture. Bankers have always designed their headquarters to inspire awe in their customers--awe for the power of money."

"They *are*awesome, Moss. I sort of like the way they've remade the landscape. The view of the prairie from the top of those buildings must be heavenly."

"Sure, the lights look pretty, but for an old hippie like me those glass houses are just an invitation to throw stones.  Man, if I had my way the banks would operate out of mud huts on riverbanks.  Mud banks.  How about it?"

"Don't deny me my magical moment, Moss.  The lights are twinkling because the bankers are happy.  Those towers aren't built of concrete or glass, Moss.  Those are mountains of money, all the credit card interest that keeps piling up."

"Right.  Every few years the banks knock down the old towers and put up even bigger ones."

"Then they lend the money to developers who want to turn apartments into hotel rooms."

Moss sighed.  "It's all too damn easy for the developers today.  In the Middle Ages it took decades to build a cathedral, and it lasted for centuries.  Now, they can assemble one of these concrete or glass monsters in a matter of weeks and, if necessary, demolish it overnight.  Nobody seems to care if it's as ugly as snot."

"From second-rate apartment to third-rate hotel, a miracle of contemporary commerce."

Moss looked at the rough concrete floor and the cracks in the slabs at the edge of the roof.  "Maybe."

I wandered over to the ledge and looked down at the street below.  "Young lawyers and accountants have already started buying up the houses around here and renting them out to waitresses, desk clerks and short-order cooks. As soon as the area gets rezoned, you watch.  The heavyweight developers will move in like tank regiments."  Shivering, I pulled my zipper up to the top of my jacket.  "When I think about the character and size of the other buildings in this neighbourhood, I wonder how the landlords ever got city hall to zone this land for an apartment complex, much less for hustles like Greenwood's hotel, restaurant and bar?"

Moss was obviously afraid of heights but he stepped forward to share my view.  "Don't know about that.  The property is too far from the city core to make any bread. The chains would never build this far out."

"According to the Honourable Daniel D. Lyon, the city is still growing."

"The boom won't last. They never do. The suburban shopping malls are already moaning to our advertising department about their sales."

"Greenwood, the hotel manager, is an accountant and he told me it will turn over lots more cash as a hotel than it did as an apartment building."

"Maybe. They'll gross a lot more, but the operating costs will climb, too. Their wage bill will go through the roof and, with the increased traffic, things will soon start to break down. The structure was never designed to be a hotel, so it won't last. But if they control costs, it could make a quick buck--for a while. After that, who knows? I guess the owners might get lucky and sell it to a chain."

"I don't understand the racket. There's an apartment shortage, but the town's hotels sit half empty all winter. How do the hotels stay in business?"

"The corporate chains do okay. They have the business class locked up tight with all the double-breasted Frequent Flyers flocking to their branches."

Stepping back from the edge, I brushed the snow off my hair. Moving under the canvass canopy over the glass door, I leaned back and crossed my arms. "The sports who run the hotel really love their games. They're the EverReady minor leaguers endlessly angling for a chance to score in the big time. You should see these two, Digger and Queenie. They're really tough competitors. They probably sponsor a minor hockey team, The Hotel Bouncers, or something."

"The Apartment Spartans?"

"The Warrior Housekeepers?"

Moss rubbed his hands. "Unfortunately, the game players aren't the only ones to suffer if they bet on the wrong horse. Or a sick building."

"To get the necessary building permits, the authorities might have to overlook little details like fire safety and inadequate elevators, right?"

Moss gave me a searching look. "Even with the current bunch, that can't be all that easy."

"As the movies teach us, shit happens. My point is that it's never the slum landlords who die in the fires or who break their legs in faulty elevators."

"Sure. Then there's the little-bitty political problem of displaced tenants."

"That's no problem, according to Dandy Lyon." I opened the door for Moss and we took a walk in the dark towards the elevators.

Moss yawned. "Don't underestimate your influence. You'll get a front-page story in tomorrow's rag. And late this afternoon, Lyon's flack spun the press gallery a story about a draft policy under review in the ministry, something about emergency shelters for the homeless."

"Just when I was beginning to think legislators had no power." I chucked the reporter under his chin. "Thanks, Moss."

"As Einstein's wives probably observed, it's all relative." Moss pushed the call button. Beside the button, I saw some half erased graffiti. Even in the dim light of the EXIT sign, the words were still visible: OCCUPIED TERRITORY: BURN GREEN WOOD! I smiled, Moss shrugged.

For some unknown reason, on the way down, the elevator doors opened on the nineteenth floor. In the hallway a housekeeper came out of one room, consulted a list on her cart, then went into the next, completely indifferent to the people watching her from the elevator.

"Have you thought much about the kind of people who lose their apartments when buildings like this get a makeover?" Moss asked.

"From canvassing, I'd say they're much like the staff in here, with most of their wages going to rent."

Moss grunted. "Ironic, isn't it, man? You lose your home but get a job working your butt off to pay for another place to sleep"

"Good line. You have a story in mind, do you, Mr. Hemingway?"

"Maybe."

I poked the down button again. "Things aren't so hot for the employees in these smaller hotels. Unlike the chains, they have no union, no pensions, and no benefits. Rose, the housekeeper I mentioned, makes only pennies above the minimum wage. Plus tips, of course. "

"Don't suppose a maid gets many tips, anyway."

"Especially, Rose. She must be the angriest woman in the West."

"Well, it's a shitty job. Wasn't that Mr. Reagan's message? If you want a job, you must compete with Mexicans or robots. Ditto from Bush and Clinton."

"Robots can make cars, but they don't buy them. Not yet anyway. And low-income workers spend everything they make, and more, on things like food, rent and cars."

Moss raised his eyes expectantly. "Did you read my feature on debt counselling?"

"That was a great read, especially the bit about the skip-tracers' convention." I leaned my head back against the wall as the elevator lumbered downwards. "You think the elevator has gone on strike?"

"Wildcat elevators? Sounds scary." Moss scratched his beard and stared at the elevator walls. "I wonder if Norman Water was one of your super-consumers?"

"Maybe so."

The elevator squeaked to a halt and the doors opened. "Do you want another Coke, or should I say, cola?" Moss asked quickly.

"No, I'm bagged. I've got to get some shuteye."

Moss had his finger poised over button number Seven. "Would cohabitation be completely out of the question? I promise not to snore."

"I'm a rolling stone, Moss. I love you but like a brother."

"What a bummer. I already have a sister."

"You also have a lover. Why don't you make up with Robyn?"

"Robyn who? I don't know any Robyn."

"Well, I do. And it's your bad memory that got you the boot. Give it up, Moss.

"Will you at least let me tell you a bedtime story?"

"Why me, Moss?"

"Because I like you, man."

"If we're going to stay friends, Moss, one thing you must do…"

"Throw myself out on the street, right? Turn myself into one of Regina's homeless souls?" He covered his face with his hands.

"That's not funny, Moss." I pulled down his hands. "I just want my privacy back. You know, a room of my own. It's time, Moss. You've got to move out, or I'll go nuts. You're not really interested in me and, if you really want a relationship, you should go and make up with Robyn." I held the elevator doors.

"Don't you want some romance in your life?"

I touched his arm. "I have a full life romancing my constituents."

"What have they got that I haven't?" Moss yanked up the zipper on his parka. "Maybe I should play hard to get, like the red neck boys in Westside."

"Wouldn't matter." I put my hand on my heart. "I shall be true to them always."

"Until they vote you out." He wagged a warning finger at me.

"Not if I can help it," I grabbed at the finger.

The reporter hid his hands. "Don't forget. Your election was a bit of a fluke. It was a squeaker and the next one will be too. "

"How could forget. I could almost quote you the results in every polling station. And, you know what? I'm going increase every one of those numbers at the next election."

"Defeat is inevitable, Regina. It happens to every politician, sooner or later."

"Good night, Moss." I gently pushed him out of the elevator, and the doors closed on his face, like the curtains on a scene in a play.

"Home, James," I said to the elevator and touched the button labelled Seven.

# Chapter Eight
## All news is old news

Friday, March 31

10:55 p.m.

I leaned on the door until the latch clicked shut. Just in case any reporters or bouncers or managers or housekeepers or handymen came scratching at the plywood, I hooked up the security chain. Peeking through the peephole, I made sure that nobody had followed me here.

The room was as hot as Harry Truman's kitchen so I turned down the thermostat to Cool and cranked open a window. I switched on the TV, but nothing happened. No matter what channel I chose, I got a blank screen. Trying the radio, I fiddled with knobs until I tuned in a local FM station. The provincial news had just started.

After hanging up my leather jacket and stowing my Docs, I scrubbed down Woolly One with a face cloth, then dabbed it dry with a towel. Stripping, I put my shirt and pantyhose into the sink. Beside the sink sat a wicker basket with little plastic vials of mouthwash, hand cream and shampoo.

The news reader led with a story about the Premier's trip to Ottawa and the environmental assessment of a big hydroelectric project down near the American border.

I picked up the tiny plastic container, twisted off the cap and poured white hotel shampoo onto my shirt and pantyhose. Turning on the tap, I watched the water run over my clothes, but the expected bubbles never appeared. The shampoo had not lathered at all. I put my hand in the water. It felt hot enough, so what was wrong? I dipped a fingertip into the white liquid and lifted it to my nose so that I could take a sniff. It didn't smell right. Shit! It was hand lotion.

The news continued with an item about oil prices.

I picked up the container marked Hand Cream, removed the top and smelled the contents. It had a scent much more like shampoo. Someone had made a mistake and mixed up the contents of the two vials. Or had they deliberately switched them as some kind of dumb joke? This was crazy or nasty or both. No real harm was done here but sometimes we depend on labels, I thought. A wrong label could be deadly. I rinsed the lotion off my wash and splashed on the shampoo.

With one ear still tuned to the news, I laundered and rinsed my clothes. Another part of my brain continued puzzling about Norman Water and his peers. Both Norman and I had been born well after the Baby Boom. Those born after the big post-war boomer cohort had been described as the most urban, educated and affluent generation in history. But the sociology grad student on my constituency executive regularly complained that boomers had secured for themselves all the best jobs, and the lion's share of public resources, leaving little for the generation that followed on their heels.

But a decade does not determine one's destiny. We can't always know how a story will turn out. By any standard, I had been a difficult kid. I read books by the dozen but hated the regimentation of the classroom. Yet I willingly submitted to the discipline of that elitist art, ballet. For years, I spent hours every day at the barre in tights and leg warmers. But, afterwards, when I rebelled and quit dancing, I wasted my nights in wild parties and sexual adventures. When they got tired of screwing around, my friends found their way back to school or into business. In myself, I discovered something different--my dead mother's political passions. No one would have predicted it. Now politics had become my life, but who knows how long that would last. Guys like "Dandy" Lyon would stop at nothing to unseat me.

Youth was supposed to be about vitality: bicycle couriers darting between the cars on downtown streets, the funky dancing girls on their way to the late night clubs, the earnest protesters at the anti-globalization rallies. I should not depend on my one sighting of the boy dead in his bathtub but Norman Water, as I imagined him, lacked any spirit. Sure, I saw lots of the kids around the district's schools who appeared passive and uncritical. They seemed to know something about everything in general, but nothing much about anything in particular. They hung out at the neighbourhood video store, but not at the library. And I'd watched the teens who wandered endlessly through the shopping malls, young urban nomads, killing time. Yet even they clung to their youth like life itself.

Norman was only a few years younger than me, but I felt so much older than that. I struggled to get Norman Water in focus, to develop a picture in my mind of the kind of person he had been. I tried to picture him as a skateboarder, a bicycle courier, or a Goth in a long black raincoat. Obviously, he wasn't a headbanger, like the ones who hassled the passersby outside the Virtual Arcade. Nor did he seem much like the skinhead in my apartment building, who liked to play Bach on his Yamaha at four in the morning. Norman would surely have had a hard time with the campus radicals or the New Agers at the expresso bars. They were talkers, not listeners, as a rule.

Maybe Norman did bear some resemblance to the listless, anorexic youths who loitered in the food malls. But they travelled in groups, and he appeared to be too much the invisible loner for that scene. Clearly, he was something of a TV addict and couch potato. A teacher remembered him as a mathematics nerd but he was surely more than that. After further consideration, I finally put my mark beside "none of the above." Forget the types, the stereotypes, the easy categories, I told myself. Save the ideology and the speeches. The point was to find out exactly who was the individual known as Norman Water?

Something on the radio caught my ear. I recognized a voice, one that sounded at the same time both familiar and strange. Surprise, surprise! Here I was talking to myself. Regina Colwell MLA is on the radio! A short item about the homeless included a clip from my performance in the House. In the broadcast, though, I had a pronounced lisp, as if I were drunk and slurring my words. Pouncing on the radio, I adjusted the tuner, censoring the lisp. With my public and private selves reunited, I returned to the bathroom to hang up my undies.

The news ended, and Madonna took over the airwaves. Too much Madonna. I switched off the radio, got into bed and turned out the light.

David Letterman was joking around in the next room. Outside in the hall a couple argued about what they had done with their key. These are ghostly echoes of the sounds overheard in hotel rooms everywhere, I thought. In the room above a "heel walker" paced the floor.

I stared at the ceiling, thinking about the boy who died in the filthy room two floors below. Mightily, I tried to identify with my constituents, but Norman Water seemed a total mystery. I found it easy to feel empathy for girls in trouble, kids with kids, penniless pensioners and the thanklessly toiling cleaners, clerks and servers. I'd work my butt off for them.

But the Norman Waters of the world--normal, ordinary kids that quit before they started--were beyond my ken. Because of this I've never been one for going quietly. Someone like me was going to have trouble getting inside the boy's head. It made me wonder what Norman wanted from life. It was hard for me to imagine him simply drifting off to his dirty little corner for a solitary death. But what happened to his family and friends? How did he die anyway? And why?

Why?

Every time I awoke that night, I asked the same question.

# Chapter Nine
# The telephone Bell called Alexander Graham

Saturday, April 1

8:08 a.m.

The telephone bell tolled not for me--not at seven, nor at eight.  The hour peacefully passed, and I slept right through it.   The front desk had forgotten my wake-up call.  I eventually stirred a few minutes after eight to the sounds of the wind rattling the windows and a vacuum cleaner whining out in the hall.  Groggy from lack of sleep, I propped myself up on my elbows.  Blinking tears to wash the grit from my eyes, I read the time on the clock radio and forced myself out of the strange bed.  Opening the curtains, I saw that yellow-grey clouds had covered the sky and yesterday's snow had ripened into rain.  With another peek at the clock, I flopped back onto the bed.

After a lazy minute, I sat up and began to plan my day.  At least I wouldn't have to waste any time deciding what to wear.  After breakfast I had to let Heather know my co-ordinates.  If no pressing constituency problems had come up overnight, I hoped to get lucky and have the day to myself.

The hotel newsstand would be sure to have at least one book worth reading.  I might even go for a swim.  It had been a long time since I'd indulged myself with a weekend break.  And if the hotel offered no better entertainment, I might just talk to the staff about Norman Water.  Overnight, the need to investigate Norman Water's death had crept up on me.  Yesterday's experiences in this weird hotel had made me determined to solve this mystery.

I padded across the carpet to the bathroom.  Without thinking, I picked up the half-empty vial of complimentary shampoo and unscrewed the cap, then, remembering my fun with false advertising last night, I smelled it first.  I didn't want another accident.  No hand cream in the hair today, thank you very much. I emptied both of last night's bottles down the sink. I could take the empty vials home and use them on my next trip out of town. Repeat after me: reduce, re-use, recycle.I turned on the taps, tested the temperature and stepped into the shower.

The spray in my face ran hot, then cold, then hot again. Supplying all the guests with their morning showers was obviously asking too much of the joint's hot water tanks. One more item to add to my scorecard of the hotel's failings. Had things really been any better when it was an apartment building? I wondered.

Just as I was done shampooing my hair and congratulating myself on avoiding one kind of accident, I immediately had another. Reaching out to pull a bath towel from the wall rack above the toilet, I knocked the towel into the toilet bowl. Swearing therapeutically, I jumped out of the shower stall and rescued the sopping cloth from the toilet. After drying myself with the spare towel, I hung them both to dry. Beside them on the shower curtain rod, my pantyhose drooped all wrinkled and sad.

I dressed. Recycle, re-use. My calves and thighs gave life to the pantyhose but my glutes could not do the same for Woolly One. Somehow skirts never hung on my hips the way they did on the dummies in the store. Worse, the body and seizing had vanished from the fabric of Woolly One. The skirt looked soft and slack now, like a hand-me-down. And it still smelled slightly of beer. My shirt, at least, looked clean. I wiped condensation off the mirror then, tucking wrinkled white cotton into Woolly One, I checked my appearance. "On reflection, Regina, you can write off the Vogue vote," I confided to my mirror image.

Smoothing the bedspread, I dumped out my wallet, sorted through the contents, then put everything back, except the cash. I had my suspicions about a couple of the hotel employees and wanted to test a hypothesis later in the day. After counting my money, I took out a pen and, in the top left-hand corner, marked all the bills with my initials and a number. That job done, I closed my eyes and massaged my eyelids. My eyeballs still ached, for want of sleep.

Showered, shampooed and dressed, I sallied forth to meet the day. Overnight, potted rubber plants had sprung up in the lobby. Touching the leaves, I identified the shrubs as that quaintly Canadian evergreen, Ficus Plasticus.

Like its neighbour, The Oasis Saloon, The Fine Diner restaurant was a recent concrete-block addition to the hotel lobby area. Although the cardboard Grand Opening sign in the window was still in the window, the restaurant looked doomed to tattiness. It had obviously been furnished by a low bidder or by the friend of a friend. The shine would soon fade from the Arborite tabletops, and the vinyl covers on the booths had probably already begun to crack at the corners. The hard-bottom, straight-back booths were the kind designed to discourage customers from lingering any longer than twenty minutes.

I sat in the bench opposite the cash register, waiting for a table and sniffing frying bacon. Cell phones chirped in the restaurant, dirty dishes clattered on their way back to the kitchen, Madonna--again!-- sang something unrecognizable from the ceiling speakers out in the lobby. Tourists trickled down for breakfast and lined up behind me. A guide with a freshly painted smile herded a tour group out of the restaurant and into the lobby to wait for a bus. Manic Man brought up the rear, sharing with the guide his thoughts on Canadian bacon. "It's the most famous thing this country produces."

The cash register sat on top of a display case full of pies and cakes. At the back of the case an angled mirror reflected not only the cream of the day's pastries, but also the legs of passers-by. As the customers stood in front of the register to pay their bills, the cashier appeared to me like a Barbie doll modeling, for brief comic moments, a succession of shorts, socks, skirts and trousers. Tourists looked so out of place in this pretend hotel. I wondered if the tourists thought the same thing about the hotel staff.

Securing a booth, I flagged down a tiny teenager, only to have the girl chased away by an older colleague. "Take off, kid! My table," growled the second server, a big-boned woman with pink hair and nails, who approached my table with her hands held out as if her nail polish was still drying. The server smoothed down her starched white apron and clipped a name tag onto the uniform bib. The tag said Holly.

"Hi." Without ever looking at me, Holly reached behind the napkin dispenser and produced the menu, a laminated card containing coloured photographs of each dish with its price and a number. To my eyes, it looked much like a precocious toddler's scrapbook except that some grown-up had obviously fixed the prices. "Fresh frozen orange juice? Coffee?" Holly inquired of the menu.

I read the card over, from top to bottom-- like an agenda. "I'll have an orange juice and a glass of water now. Coffee, later."

"Would you like another minute with the menu?"

"No need. I'll have scrambled eggs and brown toast."

"Sure you want all that cholesterol, dear?" Holly shot me a sidelong glance.

I laughed. "Sure, I'm sure. But don't butter the toast."

"Okay. One number four with dry brown coming right up." Holly breezed off through swinging doors into the kitchen.

The sales rep at the next table hungrily followed her departure. Two booths away, Lily slowly nibbled at a piece of syrup-soaked pancake, while losing herself in a Harlequin Romance. From this distance, I could not tell if Lily preferred the sappy kind of Harlequin or the spicy kind. With her frills, wrinkles and fluffy hair, Lily came on like the stereotypical spinster, but I wondered if she was happy playing that role. She looked as content as could be with her breakfast and her book. Perhaps she had the right idea. The Lily White path to enlightenment: turn on the fantasy and tune out the politics--except for her feminist moments, when there was a female candidate on the ballot.

Lily glanced up and caught me staring at her. I gave Lily a brazen salute. Lifting her paper serviette, Lily responded with a wan smile and a little wave, then meekly shifted the white flag to dab her lips, before retreating to her novel.

Inspired by Lily's example of an orderly life, I pulled a napkin out the dispenser and made a list: 1) Check the newsstand for: toiletries, toothbrush, toothpaste, hairbrush, swimsuit and reading material--a paperback or a newspaper

2) Call Heather at the constituency office

3) Go for a swim

4) Scan the news; read a book

5) Chat with the hotel staff: Bud, Rose, Lily. Queenie maybe? Greenwood again? And Norman Water's friends. If he has any.

Holly returned with the eggs. She glanced back at the kitchen as she put down the food, and a mess of hash browns scooted off the plate. When she marched off without noticing, I was meanly tempted to leave them there. But after a moment my uptight upbringing took over, and I scraped them off the Arborite with a spoon.

I ate, carefully separating with my fork the yellowish white stew from the glistening grey hash browns on the side of the plate. By the time I'd finished the eggs, the breakfast crowd had thinned somewhat, and Holly was making the rounds with a fresh pot of coffee. I watched as she visited each of her customers, arriving eventually at Lily's table. Without asking if she wanted any, the server leaned over to refill the clerk's cup. Just as Holly started to pour, Lily absentmindedly moved her cup, so that hot coffee splashed into the saucer and onto the table.

"Holly!" Lily protested and started soaking up the spill with her serviette.

"Don't get your knickers in a knot." Holly set down the pot.

"Knickers in a knot?"

"Relax. Your problem is that you've always been told that six inches looks like this," Holly held her hand up to Lily's face, her thumb and forefinger an inch apart. "You've been getting the short end of the stick, Lily."

Blushing beneath her powder, Lily quickly buried her head in her book.

"What are you reading, anyway?" Before Lily could object, Holly lifted the book out of Lily's hands. Holly scanned the title, then handed it back.

Lily looked hurt, but answered anyway. "It's about a Swedish nurse down in Central America, an army colonel and a Jesuit priest."

"Two bones and a dog, eh? Ever been down to Latin America, Lily?"

Lily glanced up, then down again. "No. You?"

"Oh, sure, like I could afford to pop down there on my days off. I just love Mexico, that whole area, the beaches, the tequila, everything--at least what I've seen of it on TV."

Sulking, Lily fixed her eyes on the fine print of her novel.

Holly shrugged, picked up the coffee-pot and moved on. Laying the bill down on my table, she asked, "Will that be all, dear?"

"A coffee, please." I turned over my cup.

Holly picked up my plate. "How was your meal?"

"To tell you the truth, the eggs were cold."

"I never touch eggs. Hey, you didn't eat your hash browns."

"No."

"Nobody does. Maybe they should drop them from the menu, eh?'"

I covered the greasy potatoes with a paper napkin. "Have you worked here long?"

Holly filled my cup, then sat down, side-saddle, on the seat opposite. With her butt ambiguously in the booth but her feet still in the aisle, Holly obviously had only a minute to share with me. "I'm new since January, but I only work weekends. Monday to Friday, I lug boxes down at the jean factory, but they're talking layoffs, so I got another job--just in case. You never know, eh? Like we all say--I'm only doing it until something better comes along." She parked the coffee-pot to fiddle with a gold-plated Age of Aquarius earring. Her planets aligned, Holly started to stack my dirty dishes.

I lifted my coffee with both hands, enjoying the heat the cup conveyed to my fingertips. "Which job do you like best?" I asked.

"Should have been a flight attendant. I would have had a rich stud waiting for me at every airport." Holly lifted one hand to pat her pink hair and cackled wickedly. "Basically the same job as here, I suppose, but classier. Waitressing's okay, it's just the customers I can't stand."

I laughed obligingly. "Did you know Norman Water?"

"The one who died?" Holly rested her chin in her hand. "Not really. I don't think he's been in here since I started. Not even for a coffee."

"Really? You're saying that he hadn't been in to eat for three months?"

Holly considered the question for a moment. "No, I never saw the guy."

"In all that time, you never even met him once?"

"No, but I heard the cooks talk about him lots."

I lowered my cup to the saucer. "You have?"

"Not only about him dying and all. Other stuff, too. Kohl has lots of funny stories about him."

"Coal?"

"Herb Kohl, K-O-H-L. He's the chef. Over there, at the staff table."

Looking across the room, I saw a florid-faced fellow in a food-splattered uniform having coffee with another kitchen worker. "The flushed-looking one with drooping moustache?"

Holly nodded.  "That's him."

The chef laughed at something and ran his hands through his long lank hair.  He glanced across the room and caught me looking his way.  He smiled and waved at me with a meaty paw.  I returned the greeting with a professional smile, then turned my attention back to Holly.

"Kohl tells a great story about Norman working as a dishwasher."

"A dishwasher?"

"Yeah.  Once upon a time, as my Ma used to say, the kid clean forgot to rinse the dishes, and half our lunch customers got the runs."

"Yes, that would definitely be bad for business."  I drained my cup and set it straight in my saucer, the handle at three o'clock, just the way Dad had taught me.

"Kohl didn't give a fiddle.  He thought it was funny."

"But not Greenwood?"  I cast a glance in the direction of the mustachioed cook.

"You know him?"  Holly looked mildly concerned.

"We've met.  So, did Kohl fire Norman?"

"Don't think so.  I figure Kohl kind of liked him.  He said he'd never seen anyone so happy beavering away at a dead-end job."

"Norman liked washing dishes?"  I tried to visualize the boy I'd seen in the bath, bent over a steaming sink.

"I guess so.  Kohl says Norman was six parts klutz, but he didn't seem to mind the boy."  Holly tugged at her ear lobe.  "Guess they had to let him go when people got sick."

"I guess.  Still, anyone can make a mistake."

"Not in the food business.  Those health inspectors will shut you down just like that."  Holly snapped her fingers.  "Padlock the doors, boys."

"Suppose so." I neatly folded my tissue-paper list.

Holly lifted the coffee-pot. "Uh, oh, Boss Alert. I'm out of here."

Turning around, I saw Greenwood and Queenie striding into the restaurant. The Manager-General was dressed for the ski slopes, in formfitting racing gear by Tommy Hilfiger. His assistant wore Spandex gym wear. Both marched in as if they were all business and headed straight for a summit conference at the staff table.

With a playful body slam, Queenie forced Kohl to move over and make room in the booth. The cook responded by punching the bouncer on the arm. Laughing, Greenwood lifted his head, and fluorescent light from the ceiling fixtures flashed off his glasses. It looked like managerial bonding session or a pre-game huddle.

Then the managers all began to talk at once, each trying to drown out the others. As Holly leaned over the table to fill their coffee cups, Greenwood slashed a finger across his throat and the group fell silent. The boss leaned towards the other two and began counting off points on his fingers. Queenie protested and Greenwood raised his voice but I could not make out what they were saying. Stealing a glance at this rambunctious group Lily slid her book off the table, down onto her lap, out of their sight. I watched as Queenie shook her head, Kohl stole glances my way and Greenwood wagged a finger at both of them.

I stuffed the list of things to do in my pocket and picked up my bill. Double-checking the total, I discovered that Holly had charged me for a second cup of coffee. Taking my pen, I put a line through the charge, deducted the price of a coffee, then added a fifteen per cent tip. Kohl waved good-bye as I left. Greenwood merely glanced over his shoulder at me, and made some remark to Queenie, then quickly looked away. How to Make a Girl Feel Welcome, by Digger Greenwood, C.A. But, hey, it's better than being totally ignored.

# Chapter Ten
# For a bad time call Regina Colwell--427-2292

Saturday, April 1

9:31 a.m.

Looking up from my list, I noted the pay phone on the wall and decided to call my office from the lobby rather than jogging all the way up to my room. Sometimes, I think about getting a cell phone but never seriously. After a couple of rings, Heather answered in her sluggish, morning-after burr. "Hello, love, I've got the office open, but we've no customers yet, how are you by the way, and tell me what happened yesterday."

I pictured Heather in her usual Saturday attitude, lolling on the waiting-room couch, with an arm over her eyes and the phone nestled in the crook of her neck. Heather had been with me from the start. We'd met back in the days when I was still doing the club scene and we'd hung out together sometimes. When my campaign headquarters opened she surprised the hell out of me by volunteering to run the office. What she lacked in administrative skills, she made up for with amazing energy. When she was not organizing bulk mailings or typing press releases, she was out knocking on doors. By election day, she had canvassed more polls than anyone except me. Heather cared. She was passionate.

"What about the dead person?"

"A young guy. He died in his bath."

"Gross. Did he bang his head or slit his wrists or what?"

"The coroner doesn't seem to know. If he does, he's not saying."

"So, was he good-looking?" Heather asked

"The coroner?"

"No! I'd never, ever date a coroner; the boy, was he cute?"

"He looked very thin." An image of Norman's corpse zipped across my brain. "Very thin."

Heather stifled a yawn. "You cannot be too thin, they say."

"In this case, I think they'd be dead wrong. His hair was long and dirty, as if he hadn't washed it for a long time."

"I thought you said they found him in his bath."

"Strange, eh? And he had my number written on his hand."

"That's not so strange; boys do that a lot."

"They do? Maybe with your number, not with mine. Can you check the files for his name?"

"It'll take me a minute because I haven't turned on Eve to check the e-mails yet. Do you want me to phone you back after she's booted up?"

"I'll hold, okay."

"Say, do you want me to fix you up after I finish?"

"Fix me up?"

"With a date for tonight. How about Hightucker? He's a hottie. If you're not interested, I might be."

"He's married."

"Regina, you're so old-fashioned. I'm certain he fancies you."

"I'm only interested in Norman Water at the moment." In order not to obstruct a carpenter with an armful of wood scraps, I pressed my back to the wall, stretching the telephone cord to the limit and twisting my head to keep the instrument at my ear.

Their project complete, the builders were finally cleaning up their job site. Greenwood came out of the restaurant to supervise as they loaded their odds and ends of wood, wire and plastic into a van parked outside in the rain. The manager glanced my way a couple of times, but when I tried to catch his eye he looked right through me. He seemed to have nothing useful to contribute to the work of the builders. Yet, for some reason, he appeared to be hanging about the lobby. Was he waiting for something? For me, perhaps?

Heather came back on the line. "Okay. Water, Norman. One entry."

I lowered my voice to a whisper. "What does it say?"

"Not much, except that he called for some info back in December."

"What kind of info?"

Heather typed something on the keyboard. "Doesn't say."

"Damn! Who took the call?"

"I did."

Straining to keep my voice under control, I pressed my assistant, "Do you remember anything about the call?"

Cornered, Heather put up a bureaucratic shield. "No, Regina, the information must have been something very routine; otherwise, I would have made a note, then followed up with a letter for your signature."

"You didn't make any notes? None at all?" I tried to keep my voice down, but my tone betrayed my irritation.

"No, I opened a file and logged the call, that's all, normal procedure."

"How is it that we have his name?"

"He must have left his name on the after-hours answering machine."

"Did he leave his number, too?"

"Yeah.  The Apartment Hotel, Room 565."

"Five-six-five?  Are you sure?"

"Sorry, five-ought-five.  It's too early in the day, so my eyes aren't open yet."

"Anything else?"

"Nothing, except that I must have answered his question right away.  If not, I would definitely have made a note to follow it up."

Bringing the mouthpiece close to my lips, I pleaded with Heather, "Do you remember anything about the call?  Anything at all?"

"Maybe if I heard him again."

"That would be just a *little* hard to arrange."

"Right.  I'll rack my brain to see what comes up."

"Anything you can remember about the guy."  I leaned my head against the coin box.  "Anything at all."

"Listen, between our two offices, we get a hundred calls a week.  It could have been any one of a hundred routine questions: Do you have the street address for city hall?  Or, our absentee MP's unlisted phone number?  Or, does Ms. Colwell agree with gun registration or capital punishment for child rapists?  I send out the usual form letter on questions like that.  If they just want to know your stand on some issue, and if I know, I tell them.  If not, I promise you'll get back to them.  You know I refer anything tricky to you."

"Do you remember anything about his speech?  The tone of his voice?  His accent?  Vocabulary?"

"Look, boss, you're making me feel like a real idiot."

I closed my eyes for a second.  "That is not my intention.  Really."  I took a deep breath.  "I'm sorry.  Maybe we need a new procedure."

After a strained silence, Heather spoke.  "Maybe you need a new assistant."

"Of course not. I type like a third-world dictator, and I couldn't function without you. How would I know when to eat or where to shop for clothes?"

Heather laughed. "It's my fault. I was up late last night. Very late."

"Oh? So what time did you get to bed?"

"I got to bed early enough, but he wouldn't let me sleep until damn near dawn."

"Lucky you." I mentally compared Heather's Friday night of the Man with the Van to the one I had with Moss.

"Lucky him, you mean."

"Right. Call me if there's anything you can't handle."

"At home?"

"At The Apartment Hotel. I stayed here last night."

"The Apartment Hotel? What, may I ask, are you doing there, still?"

"Guess you could say I'm having a naughty weekend."

"Regina! That's not like the political you, love."

"A naughty weekend, doing nothing, all by myself. Room 701, clock radio, lukewarm and cold running water, pay TV and all the greasy hash-browns you could ever want."

"Well, you haven't had a day off since the election, so it's time for some fun, although that joint would nay do it for me--too, too boring!"

"Thanks, Heather. By the way, guess who I ran into over here?"

"No idea, but do I get three guesses, and is there a prize?"

"No prize, I'm afraid; Bud Budinski."

"Buddy, my old buddy, that pest!"

"He works here."

"Of course he does. That's right, I filled out the application form for him. How's he doing? We haven't seen him for weeks. Thank the Lord."

I held my news for a beat, savouring the moment. "He wants a raise."

"Uh, oh."

"It's okay. I'll talk to his boss." I looked around. People drifted across the lobby and out the front door. A few heads bobbed at the desk, resting their bags on the carpet while they settled their accounts. Propped up against the front counter, Greenwood watched them go by. He offered the guests no help with their luggage, nor did he assist Lily with her paperwork. Occasionally though, he spoke to her, out the side of his mouth. But Greenwood seemed to have fixed his gaze on the lobby phone, not his clerk. I wondered again if he was waiting for me, and if so, why.

"I'll speak with him, right away."

"Do you want me to open a case file?"

"Yes. Do that. Okay, I'll catch you later."

I hung up the phone and walked over to the front desk where the hotel manager lounged, posing strikingly, as the daring downhill champ. If the dweeb had planned to impress me, the background music piping over the ceiling speakers totally ruined the effect. To a veteran of fifteen years of ballet classes, nothing surprises me when it comes to dance music, but the idea of skiing to Madonna's "Like a Virgin" seemed slightly comical. For the hell of it, I stood before the manager, my feet in fifth position, with a smirk on my face. "Good morning, Mr. Greenwood. Amazing outfit." I touched the Tommy Hilfiger sleeve, then punched him gently on the arm. "You like sports, don't you, sport." While I was amused at the inappropriateness of the costume, I had to admit that he looked very good in it.

"Sports?"

"Playing games."

Greenwood pulled off his glasses and peered at my face. "Speaking of games, Regina, I hope you won't be bothering the staff with any silly questions during your short stay here."

Lily ducked out of sight behind the display of travel brochures.

Leaning forward, I put my face within an inch of Greenwood's and grinned like an idiot. "Good morning, Ms. Colwell. Did you sleep well?" Like Queenie, he reeked of Brut.

Greenwood put on his glasses. "Comrade, I'm surprised at you. That sucky stuff doesn't impress anybody any more. You want a room, and you can pay for it, then I have one for rent. Let's make a deal. It's business pure and simple." Abruptly, Greenwood turned away.

I followed him. "It didn't seem so simple to me, last night."

Greenwood walked to the front door and posed as the mysterious stranger staring out at the rain. Sneaking up behind him, I whispered in his ear.

"Last night, I tried using your complimentary shampoo. It didn't work too well. The bottle was filled with hand lotion."

Greenwood looked back and frowned. "Those freebies aren't worth the trouble. When the supply runs out, I'm gonna drop 'em. Like I said: Keep it simple."

"So what's the point of the pure-and-simple business? Money?"

"Nah. Money is just a way of keeping score. Winning is the thing, the only thing." Greenwood turned on his heels again and deked by me.

I caught up to him in front of the newsstand. "What about the losers?"

"You have some particular loser in mind?" Greenwood paused, blinking.

"How about Norman Water?"

"What about Water?"

"How about: When did he work here?"

Greenwood squinted through his private windows. "He was on the payroll for a couple of months last fall. September and October, I think."

Returning his off-putting stare, I asked, "As a dishwasher?"

"Not exactly. He started on the front desk, but that didn't work out. So then he helped in the kitchen for a month or so. His last posting was as a handyman." Greenwood took off again, faking first to the right, then taking off to the left.

I gave chase. "What 'didn't work out' in the desk job?"

Greenwood turned his back on me and started to move off. "Cash, reservations, you name it."

I stepped in front of him, blocking his way. "Norman stole?"

"Nah." Greenwood tried walking around me. "Nothing like that. He just couldn't balance his drawer when he cashed out after a shift. Usually left a mess for me to straighten out."

I jumped in front, walking backwards to keep him in my sights. "What went wrong with the reservations?"

"Oh, you know: Overbooking one day, under-booking the next. Lily did her best to train him, but no luck." Greenwood looked to Lily for confirmation, which she gave with a tiny nod.

"So you transferred him to the kitchen?"

"I decided to give him a second chance."

"That was very humane of you."

"Norman didn't seem to think so."  Greenwood started moving off.

I intercepted him again.  "Oh?"

"He screwed up there too." Greenwood tried to out-stare me.

"How?"  I held the man's gaze, while he considered his reply.

"I don't think there's any point in talking about that."  He tried to evade me by shuffling to his right.

Keeping pace, step by step, I gave chase. "What?  When the people got sick?  Was that it?"

"Someone has been talking," he said over his shoulder, loud enough for Lily to hear.

"So what.  Tell me what happened."  I took his arm.

He twisted away from me.  "When?"

"When he left the soap on the dishes."

Glancing at the restaurant, he gave me a pained smile.  "It cost us a few customers.  I'll admit that."

"They got sick, I heard?"  I tugged at his sleeve.  "Eh?"

"Yes, they did."

"So what happened to the handyman job?"

"He wasn't up to it." Greenwood pressed himself against the front counter, his back to me, like a toddler playing hide-and-seek.

I tapped him on the shoulder. "What do you mean?"

"He didn't have the skills," he said between gritted teeth.

Standing beside him, I leaned back, trying to get a fix on the man's face.  "Skills?"

"Sure. You have to know how to change a fuse, fix a dripping tap, and repair a window." Greenwood's voice rose an octave.

"Unplug a toilet?"

"That's right." Greenwood fixed his eyes on the far wall.

"Why not use electricians and plumbers?"

He turned his back on me again. "Too bloody expensive."

Relentless, I planted myself in his face again. "But they have the skills, don't they?"

"Sure, but who can afford that mob? Only use tradesmen for the big jobs--the ones the government inspectors buzz around. That's my advice."

"Like hotel renovations? Ordinarily you use cheap labour? The cheaper the better?"

"You got it."

"You're an accountant. Would you recommend that I get a professional bean counter do my tax return or should I save money and get my Dad to do it? "

Greenwood said nothing.

"If you found Water so useless, why did you give him so many jobs?"

"He had bills to pay."

"Bills to pay? For his room?"

"For a start, but that's not the whole story. There's a lot more to it."

"He couldn't keep a job, but he did manage to hang onto his room?"

Greenwood lowered his eyes, nodding slowly.

"Did you fire him?"

"He was a lousy worker.  Terrible.  A complete washout."

"A loser?"

"A total loser."

Confronting him again, I tried to make eye contact.  "Then, why did you hire him in the first place?"

"He owed us money.  It was a way for him to pay it back.  I already told you that. There's no free lunch."  He lifted his chin, like the statesman on the news, before returning the goggles to his nose.

"Does that philosophy include government handouts like so-called employment training programs?"

Greenwood blinked behind the glasses.  "So, Buddy has been talking out of school, has he?"

"Don't tell me that you replaced Norman with Bud?"

"Yes and no.  We hired Bud after we let Norman go."

"Because Bud was more skilled?"

"Yes.  No, I don't mean that.  We're in the process of training Buddy. Queenie and me."

"Was Norman on the Employment Training Program too?"

"Not eligible.  He was a high-school graduate."

I shook my head in disbelief.  Greenwood responded with a raised eyebrow.

"Tell me, Mr. Greenwood, is Rose part of Bud's training team too?"

"Sure, Rose, too.  She's very good at what she does.  Why all the questions about Bud and Norman?  What's it to you, anyway?  Are you related or just plain nosy?"

"Norman was a constituent."

"Lost a vote, eh?" Cool Hand Greenwood propped himself up against the counter again. "What about Buddy?"

"Yes, he's a constituent, too." I leaned on the counter, aping the manager's pose. "And, by the way, he wants a raise."

Greenwood's eyebrows shot up. "A raise! You must be out of your warped pinko mind! He doesn't bloody well earn what he gets now."

"So, will you keep him on, when the training money runs out?"

"That depends."

"On what?"

"Costs and benefits. Costs and benefits."

I straightened up. The pas de deux was over. "Thanks for the waltz around the lobby. It has been very weird following you around, Mr. Greenwood, a madly romantic experience, something to remember in my dotage."

Greenwood the visionary looked off into the distance.

Like one of the boys, I playfully punched his arm again. "I fear you will be very lonely in your old age, Digger Greenwood."

"Lonely, but rich. Balls to sharing-and-caring. I want everything I can get. I'm going to turn this place into a bloody money machine, Regina. I have a game plan. Renovate one floor at a time, from top to bottom, finishing in the lobby. I'm one yard from the goal line, and I bloody well don't intend to punt."

I licked my finger, held it in the air for a second and shrugged. "Well, coach, you'll have to excuse me. I have to go and dream up some new laws."

"And get more people killed."

I stopped in my tracks. "What did you say?"

Greenwood pushed his glasses up his nose. "Nothing."

I did a half-turn. "You like feminist music, eh?"

"Feminist?"

"Madonna?" I pointed at the overhead speaker.

"Madonna's my kind of girl. If you weren't so mouthy, I could go for you too."

"You are a very odd individual, Mr. Greenwood."

"Sure, Regina. Give my regards to the Central Committee." Greenwood grinned, so pleased to have had the last word.

Lily smiled fleetingly, then bowed her neck to her toil.

# Chapter Eleven
# Queenie for king!

Saturday, April 1

10:30 a.m.

Shopping list in hand, I headed for the little newsstand by the elevators. Stepping through the entrance, I caught a whiff of Brut and almost walked right out again. In the far corner stood Miss Roid Rage 2000, Queenie De Lis. She was idly flipping through the pages of a muscle magazine, completely immune to the hostile vibes from the slight South Asian woman behind the cash register. I nodded to the shopkeeper and concentrated on my shopping, taking care to avoid eye contact with the bouncer.

All around me were brightly coloured packages of relentlessly advertised products, silently screaming, "Buy me! Buy me!" I hate hype but I took a sober second look at the news-stand's wares. My attitude didn't exactly qualify as sales resistance, but at a glance I still saw practically nothing in the shop that I really wanted, much less needed. "Such a poor consumer," I could hear my opponents complain. "That Regina Colwell does dick-all to keep money circulating in the local economy."

Stepping back, my eyes slowly scanned the shelves again, tracking past the brand names that shouted out at me from the displays, blinking at the hot reds, the loud yellows and the bold black print on the labels, in search of the items on my list. From the toiletries' shelf, I picked out a toothbrush, some toothpaste, a hairbrush and a little package of Kleenex.

On a rack at the back, I was surprised to find not only a T-shirt and pantyhose in my size but also a small one-piece swimsuit that might just fit. The swimsuit was an electric-green item cut high on the sides. I held it up to my body. Glancing up, I caught Queenie De Lis giving me the eye. Folding the swimsuit, I stuck it under my arm. If there had been any choice, I would likely have chosen neither the colour nor the cut. Still, I counted myself lucky to find anything at all.

I added the local daily and a *Globe and Mail*to my bundle, then checked out the bookrack. The paperback writers on display represented that exclusive club, the Best Sellers. Stephen King, Faye Kellerman, Elmore Leonard, Ruth Rendell and V.C. Andrews lined up alongside Louis L'amour and Danielle Steele. The rack had no room for any other scribblers, strictly the Continental Top Forty.

Figuring that my luck had run out, I quit the bookrack but decided to ask the shopkeeper if she had anything else in stock. I coughed stagily, and the South Asian woman, who had been busy stocking shelves with aspirins and combs, climbed down off her stool.

"Excuse me, do you have any non-fiction?"

The shopkeeper smiled apologetically. "Sorry. We carry only what the distributor sends us."

"How about Canadian fiction?"

"So sorry. We don't carry Canadian novels because the franchiser says they don't sell. Wait a minute, though." With a furtive look, she reached under the counter and produced a dog-eared paperback. "I happen to have one of my own here. It's a Michael Ondaatje and I just finished it. You can have that if you like."

I read the title aloud, "*Coming Through Slaughter.*"

"It's wonderful," said the shopkeeper. "It's about Buddy Bolden, a New Orleans jazz musician. Do you like jazz?"

"Yes, it's a great book but I've already read it. Thanks."

The shopkeeper reached under the counter again. "And I have Linda McQuaig's *Shooting the Hippo.*

"Great. I'm willing to buy that from you."

The shopkeeper considered my offer for a moment. "No, thank you, I couldn't accept money for the book came to me as a gift. When you're finished, please give it to someone else." She placed the book onto the counter and reverently pushed it towards me.

Something about the moment, the formality as much as the generosity, impelled me to bow to the donor as I received the shopkeeper's gift. Putting the book into my pocket with one hand, I passed over my purchases with the other. Up from the underground economy, down to business as usual.

"Will there be anything else?" The shopkeeper rang up my purchases and stuffed them into a plastic bag.

"Thank you, no." Handing over my money, I heard a footfall behind me, got a blast of Brut and glanced around to find Queenie on my tail.

"I do hope you won't be making yourself too awfully comfortable." Queenie eyed my acquisitions.

I picked up my shopping and turned to face the hotel's bouncer. "Queenie! How are you? Long time, no see. It's Regina Colwell. Regina, Queenie, Queenie, Regina: With names like ours we should be friends, eh?"

"To repeat: Don't get too comfortable here."

"Oh, I wouldn't worry about that, Queenie. I seriously doubt if any sane person could ever be completely comfortable in this joint--something about the atmosphere."

"I'm sorry you feel this, but that ought not to be a problem after today." Queenie pointedly lowered her eyes to size up my breasts.

I cradled my shopping bag in my arms, blocking her view. "Oh dear. Why not?"

"Greenwood told me to tell you: There'll be no room for you tonight. It's too bad, but we are fully booked." Queenie continued to make a point of running her eyes over my body rather than looking me in the face.

In a futile attempt to embarrass Queenie, I responded in kind, scoping my sights down to her belt, where she had a paging device attached next to the buckle. She had arranged the pager so that it hung, like a codpiece, right over the front seam on her Spandex shorts. I chuckled and blew a strand of hair out of my eyes. "I talked to Greenwood just minutes ago, but he didn't say a thing to me, and, it's hard to believe that he has a full house."

"At breakfast today, he told me to give you the news."

I focused on the pager dangling from Queenie's belt and tried not to laugh. "Why couldn't he tell me himself?"

Finally getting the message, Queenie lifted her eyes to my face. "Because that's my job," she said with a touch of petulance and nudged her way past me to the counter.

I tapped Queenie on the shoulder. She swung round, bumping my shopping bag as she turned. I took a backward step then transferred my attention to the heavy's non-stop eyebrows. "Kicking people out of the hotel, that's your job?"

"Certainly."

"Well, you do take pride in your work. That's something, I guess."

Sucking her teeth, Queenie considered her reply. She slapped a pair of muscle magazines on the counter. No *Ms.*, no *Fortune* or *Cosmopolitan* for the cross-dressing lady.

"Right. It's my job, and I'm frightfully good at it."

I rolled my eyes. "God, this must be the dumbest hotel ever created."

Queenie looked down her nose at me. "It makes money."

"I hope so, because it sure doesn't make sense. Hotels are supposed to make people feel welcome, but how can you do that when the staff are all so miserable?"

"Miserable?"

"Miserable: unhappy, sad, gloomy, depressed, mournful, frustrated, angry."

"Who says they're unhappy? I'll give them something to be unhappy about. Who's been talking to you? Rose? Fern? Lily? Old Holly in the diner?" Puffing up her chest, Queenie's arms rose from her sides like stunted wings.

"Queenie, would you be an absolutely fabulous darling and give Greenwood a message from me? Tell him that I'm rather a stubborn sort of person and, if you were not so eager to get rid of me, I would not be so determined to stay."

"Tell him yourself."

"Okay."

Queenie snatched up her stuff. "Charge it," she snarled at the shopkeeper.

The shopper and the shopkeeper exchanged looks. A tense moment.

I stayed out of it. But when Queenie turned away, I couldn't help calling her back.

"What about my room anyway? The hotel sure doesn't look very full."

"We have reservations." She lurched towards the door.

"So have I, sister. So have I. But, worse comes to worst, I could always stay in Norman Water's room." The suggestion had been a spur of the moment thing, a joke really, but once articulated it didn't seem like a totally absurd notion. Not totally.

"Impossible." Queenie planted herself at the door, blocking my exit.

Well, let's see how far I can take this. I put my bag down, ready to wait her out. "Why not?"

"The cops haven't finished with it, yet."

"That's okay. I'll call them."

"There's absolutely no furniture in the room."

"Put it back then." I spoke as I might to a child.

"Can't be done."

"Why not?"

"It's not here."

"Where is it?"

"Being cleaned."

I shot a quick glance at the bouncer's eyes. "It got dirty?"

"Well," Queenie chuckled, "you might say that Norman found himself in a bit of hot water."

"What does that mean exactly?"

"He had his fun, but when the bill came, he could not pay." Queenie leaned forward, imposing her pectorals on my face.

Apparently, we both loved to fight but my game was verbal combat and I had better be careful to stick to that. "You're talking riddles. I don't need all the furniture. Just get me a spare bed."

"The beds have all been booked. In any event, the room is a pigsty."

"So clean it," I said, very much the patient teacher.

"It's a very big job."

"Well, you're a very big person," I noted with a nod to her pecs. "Why don't you do it?"

She sucked air through her teeth. "Have your swim, if you must. Then, you really ought to pack your bags."

I hefted the plastic bag containing my toiletries, swimsuit, pantyhose, T-shirt and newspapers and waved it in her face. "How soon they forget. I'm packed, already. As far as you're concerned, I have all my worldly possessions right here."

Queenie smiled triumphantly. "Good. Then you can check out at once."

"No. I don't see why I should give up my room until the hotel is full. Do what you have to do. Put me on a waiting list or something. I'm not moving until you have sold every room in the house for tonight. Okay?"

The pager started to beep. Queenie grabbed at the machine with both hands and choked off the sound. Lifting her head, she scowled at me. "Greenwood won't like it."

"Tell him to talk to me. I'll meet him by the front counter. At high noon."

Queenie licked her lips. "Do you know something? You are a real pain in the ass."

"A royal pain? Thanks. I work at it." I hoisted my sack and headed for my seventh heaven. I thought I may as well hang out there until I know whether I would be staying or not. How strange that I would now count another night in this dump as a major victory.

# Chapter Twelve
## Digger even counts ants--he's an accountant"

Saturday, April 1

11:59 a.m.

I parked myself at the front desk beside a wire rack of tourist brochures and maps. Nodding at Greenwood and Lily, I inhaled a whiff of fresh varnish and waited for the wall clock to strike twelve. Of course, the clock in question had neither a bell nor a striker, so the noontime coming was a bit anti-climactic. The clock made no audible tick, just a visible flip. The digital numbers 12:00 rolled over, and time passed. Suddenly, it was afternoon. "How are you today, Ms. White? And good afternoon to you, Digger Greenwood."

Lily peeked up from her work to give me the fastest smile in the West. One blink and I would have missed it.

A moment later, Greenwood raised his head. He peered at Lily, then at me, but he never saw a thing. Perhaps because of the pencil between his teeth, he did not extend greetings or crack a smile either. Instead, he returned to his papers, his fingers racing up and down the numbers on the printout in front of him, his face the picture of professional concentration. He double-checked the total at the bottom of a column of figures, ticked it with his pencil and looked up. "We're waiting for a big group to arrive. Don't know yet if we'll have any rooms to spare, but you're probably shit out of luck."

Lily cringed.

"That's okay. I'll wait. How large is the group?"

"A block booking for one hundred rooms. Federal government--mob of bloodsuckers--having some useless conference," Greenwood grumbled. "Unlike certain provincial types, Ottawa obviously thinks this hotel will make the grade. And I'm fine with that because now I'll get some of my tax money back."

"One hundred and one rooms," Lily added with an apologetic bow to her boss.

With a thinning of his lips, he reprimanded her for the interruption.

"What time is the group supposed to arrive?" I asked.

"What's the arrival time, Lily?" Greenwood signalled his irritation by drumming on the desk with the eraser end of his pencil.

Lily looked at the clock and wrinkled her brow. "Ten fifteen."

"Call the airline," Greenwood said in clipped tones. "The weather's not so hot. Better find out if the flights from the East have been delayed."

While I unfolded a road map and Greenwood ran his nimble fingertips down another column of figures, Lily dialled.

"Everything running on schedule. They should have been here by now, even if they took the airport bus."

Greenwood squeezed his eyes shut and put his head between his hands. "When was the reservation made?"

Lily read the reservation card and bit her lip. "September."

"September?" Greenwood's eyes opened slowly. "Did you confirm it?"

"Somebody did. It's initialed. See." Lily held up the card.

Greenwood peered at the initial, as if it were an arithmetical error. He nodded and she pulled back the card. "Who made the booking?"

Gripping the form with both hands, Lily examined it carefully. "The Prime Minister's Office," she said with awe.

"The Prime Minister's Office?" Greenwood sneered. "Sure, Lily. Sure, sure, sure. Why don't you phone them, eh?"

"The Prime Minister's Office? I can't phone the prime minister."

"Go on, Lily. He probably won't take the call himself, but go on. Do it."

Lily started to lift the receiver, then paused, her hand poised mid-air. "It's Saturday," she pleaded. "Please, Mr. Greenwood."

Greenwood stabbed his forehead with the pencil. "Phone 'em, Lily."

Lily dialled the number listed on the reservation card, one digit at a time. She listened for a few seconds, then replaced the receiver, her lower lip trembling. Lily recited the recorded message "The number you have dialled is no longer in service."

"Right!" Greenwood flipped his pencil and erased the tick at the bottom of the printout. "Who wrote up the reservation?" Greenwood's face was frozen with fury.

Studying the card again, the clerk's hand began to shake.

"Who, Lily?" he snapped.

"Norman."

Greenwood gripped the pencil in both hands. "Norman?"

"Norman."

"Too right!" Greenwood broke the pencil in half and swivelled his chair round to face me. "There you have it, Comrade. Your friend, Norman Water. At it again. Another nasty bit of sabotage. That anaemic little drip!" he snarled and threw the bits of broken pencil onto the floor.

Gently, I asked, "Does this mean I can stay the night? I know one provincial politician can't make up for one hundred federal bureaucrats but I'll do my best."

Wheeling around, Greenwood ripped off his glasses and flung them over the counter. The glasses bounced off the lobby carpet and landed in the drainage tray beneath a potted plant. An awkward moment followed during which Lily blew her nose and Greenwood blindly fumbled his way out from behind the counter.

Sheepishly, Greenwood crept across the lobby carpet to search for his spectacles. I took the man by the arm and steered him in the right direction. He let me lead him towards the pot, but he insisted on dipping his fingers into the dirty water and fishing around for his glasses. Locating them at last, he blew off leafy debris and wiped off the moisture on the lenses. Putting them on, he found that the frames were bent out of shape. So, holding the twisted spectacles up to his face, and, cursing under his breath, Greenwood disappeared around the corner to his office.

"Was that one of Norman's little jokes?" I asked Lily.

"I think so." The clerk collapsed into a chair.

"Why would he do something like that?"

"Well, I suppose Digger was always at him about empty rooms and how you had to over-book to guarantee a full house." Lily folded Norman's reservation card in half.

"What happened when all the reservations showed up?"

"That's what Norman hated; finding other rooms for all those angry customers." Lily folded the card again and dropped it into the trash can.

I leaned on the counter. "Norman Water's revenge?"

"I think so." Lily began to gather up the papers her boss had spread over the desk.

"Was this the first time he'd played tricks on you?"

"No," Lily sniffed. "It's not the worst thing he ever did, either. Once he hid the credit-card machine in the laundry room so we couldn't check anyone in or out."

"Why would he do that?" I tried to picture the boy in the bath hiding the charge card imprinter, but couldn't.

"I really don't know." Lily dabbed her eyes with a tissue. "Maybe he did it because Greenwood told him he couldn't charge anything more to his room account."

"I see." I watched Lily fussing about, sorting papers, straightening the desk, tidying the cash in the till. "Can I pay now? For tonight?"

Lily thought for a second, looked about for someone in authority, then nodded.

"And can you change an extra hundred dollar bill?"

"Of course." Lily stepped up to the cash register, smelling of damp talcum.

After handing the clerk two of my marked one-hundred-dollar notes, I switched my attention to the road map she had spread out on the counter. I traced the Trans-Canada Highway across the Prairies as Lily counted and recounted the change. The clerk handed over the money.

"Thank you. Should be $140, right?"

Lily swallowed and bobbed her head.

With a wet finger, I slowly counted out the bills onto the counter. "Twenty, forty, sixty, eighty, one hundred, one twenty, one hundred and thirty dollars. One thirty? Oh. Better count it again." I glanced at the cash register.

"No!" Lily made a grab for the money, but I snatched it away. "It must have been my mistake." The clerk dived for the cash drawer. She came up with a ten-dollar bill. "Here." She slapped down the money.

I left the note lying on the counter. Exhibit B. "Greenwood mentioned that Norman Water had trouble with both his reservations and his cash. Have I got that right, Lily?"

Over the tops of her glasses, Lily stole a quick look at her inquisitor. "'Watch the pennies or risk coming up short at the end of the day.' That's what I told him."

"Did you short-change him too, Lily?"

Lily's face twitched.

"Did you dip into Norman's cash?"

The clerk's mouth opened and closed like a goldfish, but not a sound emerged.

I sighed. "Lily, tell me what happened to the kid."

Bowing her head, Lily took a deep breath, then another and blurted it all out. "When Norman checked in, he had nothing except his credit card. Right off, he started buying clothes, ordering in Chinese food, charging restaurant meals and laundry to his room account or his credit card. He treated the card as it was the bank's responsibility, not his. Mr. Greenwood saw what was happening and offered him a way to pay it off."

"A job?"

"Yes."

"Your job?"

Her eyes on the edge of tears, Lily lifted her head slightly. "Oh, no. We had just enough clerks but...."

"But what?"

"He paid Norman less than me."

"That had you worried?"

"Of course," Lily said in a small voice.

"So, while you were training him, you dipped your fingers into his cash drawer?"

Lily's lips trembled. "Just a touch. Once or twice. To teach him a lesson about business."

"A lesson? About business? Did he have to make up the

difference?"

Lily nodded. "Yes."

"Out of his pay?"

"Yes." Lily buried her chin in her ruff.

"Did he catch on?"

"I think so."

"So he paid you back by messing up your reservation system. Is that right?"

"Suppose so."

I waited for her to say more. In the silence, a bead of sweat broke out on Lily's forehead and rolled down her cheek. Cracks began to appear in Lily's face powder.

"How long did all this last?"

"A few weeks."

"September and October?" I folded up the road map.

"He got transferred in October."

"To the kitchen?"

"Yes." Lily stood rooted to the spot, her head bowed, her fingers entwined.

I studied the ten-dollar note on the counter. For the first time, I became really aware of the artwork on the back of the bill. It showed a raptor flying over a lake with a fish in its claws. The word CANADA filled the distant sky. I wondered briefly if the bird was supposed to be an eagle. Taking out my pen, I marked the bills Lily had given me then put them away.

Lily started sobbing, so I left her to it.

Back in my room, I flopped on the bed and read Moss's story about my legislative set-to the day before. The newspaper also ran dry accounts of global warming and the melting of the polar ice cap, drought in America, desertification in Senegal and the two billion people world-wide without drinkable water. After ten minutes, I gave up. I couldn't stop wondering why Norman had called me and why he hadn't called a second time.

Later, when I went back down to the lobby, Greenwood had uprooted Lily. And he had changed his outfit. Now, in aviator goggles and a khaki survivalist outfit, he'd planted himself at the front counter, the last defender of a fort besieged. I imagine the cut-line under the picture: Digger Does Mercenary Chic: No-Frills Hotel Management.

# Chapter Thirteen
# Herb has a nose for trouble

Saturday, April 1

1:11 p.m.

I was sitting in a booth opposite the kitchen, reading the *Globe's* book section. On any other day, I would have chosen instead to go swimming but, first, I wanted to talk to Kohl. Every time the kitchen door swung open, I looked up and caught a blast of kitchen chatter, dish clatter and hot fatty smells. Finishing the book reviews, I folded the paper and waited. When at last the head cook emerged from the kitchen for a break, I got up and walked over to the staff table. Kohl watched my approach, smile lines lengthening down his ruddy cheeks.

"Mr. Kohl, I'm Regina Colwell."

"Herb, please." He sniffed once, then pinched his nostrils between his thumb and forefinger.

"May I join you for a mo? I'd like a word, if you have the time."

Kohl slid out of the booth, tugged at the hem of his uniform jacket, then bowed me into the seat opposite him. "How could anyone refuse such a lovely lady?"

"I see you follow the European tradition of hotel management."

Kohl fingered his moustache. "I'm sorry I don't understand."

"Insincere flattery." I gave him a friendly smile. "If you don't mind my saying so, you seem to embody old-world charm."

Kohl laughed, his belly quaking under his smock. "Ah, you've detected my Swiss accent."

"It's very slight but quite charming, as I said."  Keep this up, Regina, and you'll have to find some violins for the background music.

Kohl was enjoying my styling him almost as much as I did.  "Well, my limited charms are more than you'll get from most folk around here."

"Digger and Queenie?  Based on one short stay, I'd say that's true enough."

"What an amusing pair those two are.  A couple of tough customers, but they do get things done.  They're very good at what they do."

"Amazing, for sure," I said with a straight face.

"As Greenwood never tires of telling us, there's not much money in charm or polish out here.  Paris and Rome are a long way away."  Kohl gave his nose another squeeze.  "Would you care for a coffee?"

"Tea, please." I offered him a Kleenex.  "Do you have a cold."

I looked around for a server; Kohl's eyes tracked mine.  "I'll get it.  Sugar?  Lemon?  Herbal?"

"Plain, thank you."

Popping into the kitchen, Kohl returned with the ubiquitous metal teapot, the kind that usually dribbles all over the table.  Kohl poured.  His beefy paws made precise little movements as he dipped the tea bag, held the lid and filled both our cups.  In his professional hands, nothing dribbled.  Not a drop.  He managed to look both light-fingered and heavy-handed, as if somehow the fingers and hands belonged to separate bodies.  When Kohl cradled his cup, his hands clutched it like a beat cop on a cold day, but when he tipped the container to his lips his pinkie rose like a poseur at a cocktail party.

His white uniform was splattered with everything from soups to sauces and he smelled slightly of grease and pepper.  His whole appearance was an unlikely combination of bulk and delicacy.  His eyes appeared squinty, but deep smile lines fanned out from their corners.  The walrus moustache gave his face a mournful cast, but his frequent laughs instantly banished any traces of sadness. When he had lurched out of the kitchen earlier, I noticed that his arms and legs didn't move in sync. He looked as if his belly button was off-centre and the puzzle of his pieces didn't quite fit together.

"How long have you worked here?" I asked.

"Oh, a few months only." He sniffed noisily, his moustache twitching.

"Are you a local hire or an import?"

The cook paused, considering his answer. He shrugged.

Not to be put off, I asked again. "Did you come here from somewhere else?"

As if to wipe away the memory, Kohl rubbed his face with his hands, stretching the skin around his skull. "You might say local. I stumbled into the joint at the tail-end of a long tour of the city's drinking establishments. When I sobered up, I found myself in a fourth-floor room with a giant bill to pay. Now I have an unfinished staff room up on the nineteenth floor. That's progress, but not exactly what I expected when I immigrated."

"You're joking. Are you really working off a room bill?"

Kohl flicked the tip of his nose with his forefinger.

"This could be a story out of Dickens."

Kohl laughed. "It's not the poorhouse, Regina. I do get paid, and I'm always free to look for a better position--at least that's what Greenwood tells me." The chef shovelled three heaping teaspoons of sugar into his cup, added milk, blended the ingredients.

"What's it like working here?"

Kohl frowned and shrugged.

"Do you like your job?"

"Nobody has ever asked me that before.  The answer is: not much. I'm chef at the Hotel Who Gives a Damn.  We don't get many gourmands here.  Forgive me, but food is just fodder for our crowd." His hand swept the room.  "These people have no taste whatsoever. Cooking quality food for them is just not worth the trouble.  Most of them wouldn't know custard from curry.  If it's not deep fried, it's not cooked.  Then we get the cowboys who like their steaks raw, not rare.  It's not cooking they want, it's cow!  But, I'm adaptable.  I have studied the local customs.  I'll manage."  Kohl toasted me with his teacup.  "Until something better comes along."

I lifted mine in response, then settled it in the saucer.  "I hear you worked with Norman Water?"

Grinning, he wagged his finger at me. "Digger warned us you'd be asking questions about Norman."

"I don't get it.  Why would he care?"

"Worried about the bad publicity, I expect.  He doesn't want any government types crawling all over the place.  They make him nervous."

"You'd think he'd welcome the business."

"Oh, we like them as paying customers.  Love them.  Great expense accounts.  But they're not much fun when they're working.  Tax collectors, liquor inspectors, labour-standards officers, the like."

"Coroners, cops...."

"Yeah."  A cloud passed over his face then he sniffed again.  "You're not working today, are you, Miss Colwell?"

"No, I'm taking a day off, a little vacation.  But, all the same, I'm curious about what happened to Norman Water.  He was a constituent of mine."  I sipped some tea, watching Kohl as he sniffed and slurped, and grinned.  I was gambling that he would not misread my interest in him.

"Well, I have no idea what happened with him in the end.  We hadn't seen him for weeks.  Locked himself in his room and wouldn't come out." Kohl spooned more sugar into his tea.  "Imagine you or I doing that."

"Why do you think he did it?" I asked.

Kohl stirred his tea, the spoon propelled by tiny movements of his fingertips.  "Go figure?  Kids today, they do strange things."

"How do you think he died?  Did he starve, drown or what?"

"Who knows?"  Kohl tapped the spoon on the rim of his cup, then put it in his saucer.  "But I'd be surprised if he starved.  He ate like a tapeworm when he worked in my kitchen.  I don't know.  Maybe, he just gave up, quit trying, or maybe he did just quit eating.  Why?  Who knows?  Maybe he got sick?  The authorities will get to the bottom of it, I suppose."

"What was he like at work?"

"Quiet, very quiet.  Never said much, but I noticed that he kept his eyes open, watching and listening to everything.  He also had an anarchistic sense of humour."  Kohl swirled the tea in his cup, then took a long drink.

I shivered at the thought of the sugar surging around the cook's teeth, down into his stomach, into his bloodstream. "Anarchistic?  You're referring to the incident with the soapy dishes?"

"You heard about that?"

"Greenwood mentioned it.  What happened?  Was it not an accident?"

"Oh, no.  Things got a bit hairy one day.  People yelling at each other and so forth.  It's like that sometimes when it gets busy.  Anyway, I guess the waitresses were giving him a rough time about dirty dishes or not enough clean dishes or whatever.  So when the time came for the staff to take their lunch break, he handed them dishes that had not been rinsed.  He may even have put a cup of soap in their soup, but I couldn't swear by it."  Kohl chuckled at the memory. "We had a very active crew that afternoon. Never seen them move so fast."

"I thought some customers got sick."

"No," Kohl said with a firm shake of his head. "Just staff."

"You're sure? That's not the way I heard it."

"I'm certain," he insisted. "I was there. Saw it happen."

I sipped tea and watched Kohl. He cradled the cup in his huge hands, like a starving orphan with a soup bowl. Then, like a bereft fortune-teller, he smiled slightly at the bottom of my empty cup. I nodded and Kohl refilled it. "Do you recall another, similar, incident when people got sick?"

"People? You mean, customers." He pulled at his cheeks, thinking.

"Sure, customers."

"Oh yeah. Of course!" Kohl clapped his hands with glee. "It was fantastic. The mayor had these Friday prayer breakfasts. God, I hate those phoney hypocrites! One time someone, probably Norman, doped up their corn-beef hash. Those bible thumpers had the time of their lives. Thought they'd seen the Second Coming, I bet."

"The whole group got stoned? Including the mayor?"

The cook's face positively glowed at the memory. "Sure, everyone."

"That must have been quite a sight. Lucky nothing leaked out to the media." In a hushed voice, I asked, "Nobody got seriously ill, I hope."

"Nah. But one of them rear-ended a city bus on the way to work, and that ended the mayor's prayer breakfasts as far as we were concerned. No big deal. A few complaints. We lost their business, but the staff didn't mind because they were lousy tippers anyway."

"Didn't you mind?" I asked, somewhat puzzled.

"No, not me.  A most amusing incident.  You need a good laugh, now and then."

"But Norman Water got fired?"

"Not fired, demoted.  Greenwood moved him down to the basement.  Made him a handyman.  Too bad, really.  He was fun in a way, stirred things up good."

"Why would he pull such a prank?"

Kohl ran his hands through his hair.  "Beats me.  But he was full of little tricks.  One time, a waitress was fixing her make-up at the table here, and I guess Norman must have picked up her lipstick.  Anyway, he used it to paint big, sexy lips onto the seat.  A few minutes later a barmaid came along and parked her butt right on the very spot.  When she got up she had this huge red kiss printed on her ass.  Everybody killed themselves laughing.  The poor girl couldn't figure it out at all."

"I'm with the girl.  He sounds pretty dumb to me."

"Sure.  Somehow, though, I think he may have been smarter than he acted.  Possibly--just possibly--there was some method to his madness."

Holly came charging out of the kitchen loaded with a tray full of water glasses.  "Mr. Gold Earring in the Corvette is out in the alley.  He wants a word," she said to Kohl on the way by.

"Tell him I'll be right there.  Well, Miss Colwell, I must go.  Duty calls and all that.  Come and see me again."  He sniffed, clicked his heels and marched off.

"Can Bud talk to you, Regina?"

I looked up.  Bud Budinski hovered near my table in an excited state, flapping his hands and hyperventilating.  "Sure, Bud, take a seat."

Bud shook his head.  "Can't," he breathed.  "Not allowed in here."

"I don't get it.  Why not?"

"Handyman and chambermaids have to eat in the laundry room. It's the rules."

"That's ridiculous. Why?"

"Dunno. It's rules." He chewed his lip, anxious but insistent.

"Okay, Bud, I'll catch you as soon as I can."

Finishing my tea, I pondered the mysteries of lunch in the laundry room, drugs at the mayor's prayer breakfast and the chef with a major nose problem.

# Chapter Fourteen
## Don't drink the water; Sharks piss in it

Saturday, April 1

2:02 p.m.

Up in my room, I stripped, hung my clothes and pulled on my flashy
new swim suit, mugging in front of the bathroom mirror as I tugged
and stretched the material to cover more of my flesh. To my
surprise, the suit fit me perfectly. The colour was a bit shocking and
the cut exposed large patches of pale skin on my chest and thighs.
Never mind, last year's tan had almost faded away. And, anyway, I
wasn't likely to meet anybody who cared a fig about Regina
Colwell's fashion statement. Greenwood or Queenie might put me
down, but who cared what those two thought. Wrapping a towel
around my waist, I headed for the door. Just as I touched the handle,
the phone rang. I snatched it up and waited. "Is that you, Buddy?"
After a few seconds of listening to dead air I banged down the
receiver and went up to the pool at the Rooftop Garden.

Even in broad daylight, the garden failed as a pastoral setting. It
would take a bad trip to turn the space into paradise or even a Roman
bath. In plain fact, the Rooftop Garden consisted of nothing more
than a glassed-in area on the hotel roof, containing a pool plus a
dozen trees and plants of the kind that would never have survived a
day outside in a prairie winter. The decor was so totally fake that I
actually liked it.

The rain-streaked glass roof provided a blurred view of a cloudy sky.
At the south end of the area, large glass doors gave access to a
concrete patio and, leaning dangerously against the door frame, a
stack of weathered aluminum lawn chairs. Mist blanketed the glass
doors; moisture stippled the adjacent walls. A translucent bead of
moisture snaked down the pane cutting a clear path through the mist.
For a moment, until I fogged it with my breath, I could see clearly

out into the cold, grey day.

From overhead, I heard Madonna pushing her "Boy Toy" number but a damaged speaker made the singer's voice sound cracked and old.  In a corner, beside the patio doors, stood what guessed were the managers' toys: a stationary exercise bike, a sun lamp and a set of weights.   I hoped, for the sake of both the glass and the plants that Greenwood had some rules about Queenie throwing her weights around.

The pool sat square and sterile in the middle of the tiled floor, a sky-blue concrete cube filled with chemically treated water, just waiting for human definition, lifeguards or bathers, someone to separate length from breadth.  Only the ceiling lamps shining down onto the water cut the gloom.  Beneath the lights the water rippled slightly, making eerie shadows on the bottom of the pool.  Like a lake full of acid rain, the pool looked, at once, wonderfully inviting and clinically dead.

I shucked my towel and climbed down the tiled steps into the shallow water.  It felt cold and, up close, it had a sour chlorine smell, but wading in I found it pretty sweet.   I fell forward with a splash, and the sound echoed off the hard walls.  With the water lifting my legs free of the blue concrete floor, I stroked once, glided slowly, then stroked again, liberating myself from the vertical plane.

The waves lapped at my ears, muffling all airborne sounds.  Watching the shadows on the bottom, I pictured myself alone in the pool, not on the roof of a tall building but rather floating free of gravity in an airborne water bubble, way up in the sky above the city, above the storm, above it all.  Like an angel in heaven, I thought.  Daydreaming, I swam until I bumped my head on the concrete at the deep end.  Righting myself, I trod water, felt for lumps on my skull, then plunged forward again.

Under the water, I followed a seam in the concrete, came up for air, then swam another length along the bottom.  Surfacing, I settled down to a regular pattern, doing the crawl up the pool and the backstroke down.  The pool was only half the size of the YWCA's, but once I got into the rhythm my arms and legs began loosening up, the kinks in my neck unravelling. The water washed over my skin, buoying my muscles, touching every nerve, living proof to my body of its essential nature. Had Norman felt this way, in his element, as it were, in the pool he loved so much?

Over lunch hour, at the YWCA, I often swam somewhere between a kilometer and a mile. Generally, I made light work of the forty lengths but my kilometer was as boring as a budget debate. That was the trouble with swimming. One had to be mindful of the number of laps, the lane markers and the other swimmers. One had to watch out or risk an accident, like cracking my skull on the bulkhead.

Yet, the noon hour swim was the perfect alternative to power lunches, allowing as it did for few reflective moments trying to fathom the world in the lengths between the shallow and the deep. On my back, I mentally counted the lights, one to ten, then tucked and turned in the six feet of deep water. Returning, I watched the bottom approach, closer and closer, until touching the edge, I flipped over and ticked off the lights again, one, two, three, four. . . .

By the seventeenth lap, I had replayed the morning in my mind and even flashed back to the day before, an aeon ago when I existed only as a stranger on the street outside, not the insider, the Occupant, I was today. How did the story go? Norman Water, the polite prankster, went for a swim, moved into the hotel, got a job, got fired, squatted in his room and died in his bath. Meanwhile Digger Greenwood was transforming the apartment hotel into The Apartment Hotel, while Queenie De Lis showed the guests the door, Lily short-changed the tourists, Fern poured beer in their laps, Rose cursed, Kohl laughed and Bud mopped the floors. What a madhouse. But, maybe the joke was on Norman, after all. In the end, he alone seemed to have paid the ultimate price for their sins.

I could not figure out what the kid had been doing. Someone had provoked each of his practical jokes, like the phoney government reservations. No doubt he'd left more time bombs buried about the building, tricks to avenge some indignity or settle some score. But what had been the point of the lipstick kiss on the server's butt? Or drugging the Mayor's Prayer breakfast? Like his namesake element, he seemed to lose himself in his surroundings, only to reappear with his next trick, in a new form.

I touched the wall, turned and pushed off, gliding underwater, a foot below the surface. I heard all their voices: Queenie, Lily, Greenwood, Rose, Holly and Bud, talking and talking, but none of it made much sense. I heard a voice calling my name. Breaking surface, I found Bud crab-walking along the tiled deck beside the pool, talking non-stop. I swallowed a mouthful of water, pulled in my arms and slowed my kick until I was just floating along. Coughing water, I shouted at Budinski. "Bud, I said I would come and see you and I will."

Bud's mouth became a straight line across a pinched face. "Have to talk to you now."

"Bud, I can't talk to you now. I'm busy."

Swimming obviously didn't meet Bud's definition of busy. When I turned so did he. "Did you talk to Mr. Greenwood, Regina?" he asked in an anguished voice.

I rolled over on my back. "Yes, I did, as you asked."

Bud made a face. "Now Mr. Greenwood is pissed at me."

I came to a stop at the shallow end and stood up. Pulling hair away from my face, I waded towards the agitated young man. "Sorry about that Bud, but you did ask me to talk to him for you."

Like a caricature of a child in a Saturday morning cartoon, Bud stamped his foot. As his heel hit the deck, it occurred to me that I had never before seen anyone actually do this. His face melted into tears. "Gonna lose my job now," he wailed.

I reached out to him as I rose from the water but the man turned and fled as if my hand held a poisoned apple.

"Norman!" I shouted as he disappeared towards the elevators. "Norman? I mean Bud." I corrected myself. And snatching up my towel, I took off after him.

Glimpsing the man skulking in the back of the elevator, I sprinted to catch him. Bud glanced up, saw me coming and fell onto the control panel. The door closed just as I reached it. I stuck my bare foot between the rubber pads, trying to force the door open. Through the crack between the doors, I saw Bud step forward, lift his foot and stamp down hard at my toes.

I pulled my foot free--fast, but not fast enough. Bud's running shoe caught my big toe. As the pain hit, I sucked in my breath. Grabbing the injured toe with both hands, I hopped around until the hurt subsided then limped over to the other elevator and pushed the call button.

In a minute the machine arrived, I climbed aboard and sent it down to the basement. When the ride ended and the door opened, I looked out into a dark and empty, concrete corridor. I saw no sign of anyone. I got back in and punched all the numbered buttons on the control panel. At the ground floor, I popped my head out to look for Bud in the lobby area, but he was not there either.

I checked for him on the second floor, again without success. At the next floor, I got off and looked both ways, up and down the hall, but still no luck. I struck out again on the fourth floor and on the fifth but, on the sixth floor, I scored. Hitching his sweat pants, Bud plodded down the long hallway. Overweight and knock-kneed, he moved with a rolling gait, swinging each of his legs wide of the other. On the back of his tank-top, I read a faded advertisement for a local Ford dealer.

Rather than alarm him, I waited until the word Ford disappeared through the Fire Exit at the far end of the hall, then ran softly along the carpet to the door, reaching it just before the hydraulic hinge shut it tight. Looking down over the metal guard rail, I glimpsed my guy picking his way down the stairs and tiptoed after him.

He made his way down to the basement, around a dark corner through an unmarked door. Following at a discreet distance, I reached the door, turned the handle and stepped into a broom closet. At the back of the tiny room, on a drum of floor wax, Bud sat, sulking. He lifted his eyes as I arrived then, recovering from the surprise, he rushed at me, his fists swinging wildly. But before he could strike, I grabbed both of his wrists and forced his arms down to his sides. Bud struggled for a minute but to no effect. He outweighed me by at least a hundred pounds but he was weak and uncoordinated and I had no trouble restraining him. Even after I had him pinned though, the anger still burned in his eyes. "Easy, Bud, easy. Tell me what's wrong, Bud." I spoke softly, repeating his name. "Tell me, what's wrong, Bud. Please?"

His lips still quivered slightly but his body had gone limp and feeble. "The boss said your mouth is trouble. He says you're going to get me fired."

Releasing his arms, I placed my hands on his shoulders. "Listen, Bud, I'm not going to get you fired. I'm not. Haven't I always helped you with your problems? Eh?" I shook him a little to get his attention. "I'm not going to let them get rid of you without a fight. All right? Come on, look at me. Even if you did lose your job, I'd help you get another one. Wouldn't I?"

Bud licked his lips then wiped his nose with the back of his hand. "They said Bud could get into big trouble for talking to you."

Lifting his chin, I looked him in the eye. "Greenwood said that?"

"And Queenie."

"Queenie?"

"Yeah."

"Tell me something: Was Norman mad at you for taking his job?"

Snivelling, Bud looked around for some Kleenex then wiped his nose on his sleeve again. "Norman was my friend. He always let me hang out in his room and watch his TV. We'd order up pizza and pop, tea and stuff like that."

"Pizza and pop? Did you order it from the hotel restaurant?"

Bud dismissed the suggestion with a swipe of his chin. "No. They don't have pizza. We sent out for it. We did that most days."

"How did you pay for it?

Bud smiled as if he had a great secret. "Norman had a credit card. He bought lots of stuff, Nintendo games, clothes, Nikes, a boombox. Queenie told me, 'Work hard, do your job, and you can get a credit card too.'"

"Save your money, Bud. Credit cards are a rip-off. The banks charge almost twenty per cent interest on the accounts. Cash is simpler, and a lot smarter. Did Norman send out for tea too? On his credit card?"

"No, Norman had a kettle and a stove. But, after a while, they said we couldn't eat in the rooms unless it came from room service."

"That's ridiculous. Why not?"

"Rules. Greenwood rules. That's what Norman said."

"So you and Norman got along pretty well?"

"Yeah, we were good buddies. Totally."

I took Buddy's hand. "Bud, did Norman finish school? I mean did he graduate from high school? Was he, perhaps, planning to go to college? You understand me?"

"Of course I do. I'm subnormal, Regina, but I'm not an idiot."

"I'm sorry, Bud. You're right. I should have known better."

"Norman finished up high school before he came here. His ma moved down South and his pa went back East, I think. They said Norman was damn well old enough to go out on his own."

"Do you know if the family lived here a long time?"

"No, Norman said they'd only been here a year or two."

"Did Norman have any relatives here? Any brothers or sisters?"

"He was a lonely child."

"An only child?  Really?  Probably, lonely too, eh?"  I began to towel my hair.  "Did Norman like the pool?  Did he use it a lot?"

"Every day."  Bud began warming up to the exercise.  He seemed to know this was one quiz he might pass with honours.  "Until they stopped him."

"Why did they do that?"

"Because his bill got too high.  They said he couldn't swim any more."  Bud giggled into the palm of his hand.  "So, you know what happened?  Norman got mad.  He waited for a few days and then one night when it went down to twenty below, he sneaked up to the roof, he opened all the patio doors, he turned off the heat, and the pool got freezing cold.  Norman hung out until it got to be time for Queenie to finish for the day, then he closed the doors again.  So, after work, Queenie came up to go skinny dipping like she always does.  She dropped her drawers, dived into the pool and screamed blue murder.  Boy, was she surprised!  Just about froze her tits off."  Laughing like a child, Bud's eyes shone with delight at the story.

He prattled on about his favourite pizzas, videos, video games and the TV programs Norman and he watched together, while I tried to picture the friendship between these two males.  Was Norman the big brother, the protector?  What kind of companion had the superficially passive Water boy been to Bud?  Did Bud do all the talking and did Norman not mind?  A bit of Bud's chatter interrupted my thoughts.

"Norman could of had unemployment insurance but he didn't work here long enough."

"Yes, that must be right."  I looked down and noticed that since yesterday Bud had acquired a new pair of Nike Airwalkers.  Based on the newspaper ads I'd scanned these runners were one of the more expensive brands.  "Bud, do you get enough money to get by?"

"It's hard.  I have rent to pay and food to buy.  And the phone."

"I know, but do you get any extra money from anyone?"

Looking proudly at his new runners, Bud smiled to himself. "Queenie gives me tips sometimes."

"What for?"

"Re-search. She calls it research. 'Tips for tips,' she says."

"What kind of research?"

"I find out things for her."

"Like what, Bud?"

He twisted his mouth to the side. "Embarrassing stuff."

"Embarrassing stuff?"

"I can't tell you. Queenie said it's a secret."

"I see. You find out embarrassing stuff about people and she pays you for the information?"

Thinking, Bud licked his lips. "Yeah," he said finally.

"What kind of secrets, Bud?"

"I can't tell. Queenie would kill me if I told. She's a big dude!"

I thought about the kind of secrets Bud would find in the rooms of hotel guests. They were probably little private matters. But what would Queenie be doing with these secrets? Not much probably, but with Bud as her spy, she might from time to time learn something profitable. Well, there was nothing in my room they could use against me. "What do you do with the money you get from her?"

Bud grinned. "I'm saving up for a holiday. You know where?"

"Where, Bud?"

"Hollywood. I'm going down to see the starlets."

"Starlets?"

"On Sunset Boulevard.  Queenie says you can meet them right on the street."

I shook my head.  "You'd better watch your wallet if you go anywhere near Sunset Strip, Bud.  That's no place to look for love."

"How come?" Bud said, pouting.

"It's not real love, Bud.  How can I explain?  It's pretend love, it's phoney."

Bud looked downcast.

For both our sakes, I changed tack.  "Bud, think back a bit.  Do you remember telling Norman to call me?"

"No."

"Do you have any idea why he would have phoned my office?"

"No, but I told him about you."

Leaning back against the door, I adjusted the towel around my shoulders but the material was too threadbare to provide much warmth.   In the deep of my mind, an idea lurked but I could not get a line on it.  Absent-mindedly I rubbed my back with the towel.  Closing my eyes for a second, I felt a hand squeeze my breast.

I jumped, my eyes wide, knocking Bud's hand away.  "Bud, listen to me and listen good.  Don't ever do that to a woman.  Not without her permission.  You could get into big trouble.  Big trouble!"

Bud froze, then hid his face.  "Rules?"

"Rules?"  I nodded.  "That's right, Bud, rules!"

 The handyman backed away, embarrassed.  He slumped back onto the metal drum.  "Don't tell Queenie," he pleaded.

Turning the towel over to its dryer side, I wrapped myself in it once more, treasuring this meagre comfort, courtesy of the Apartment Hotel.  "Look, Bud, one day you'll meet someone you like, someone who likes you. When that happens you'll both know it. When two people like each other, they touch. If it feels right, if they feel strongly enough, they will make love. When you find the right person, you will know it, Bud."

"When?" he demanded, pouting like a spoiled brat.

I couldn't lie to the guy. "I really don't know, Bud, I don't."

"You're the one I want, Regina."

"No, Buddy, I'm not."

Bud clenched his teeth, folded his arms and turned his back on me. In that instant, I realized I'd lost him. He felt betrayed by me. Not without some regret, I realized that Mr. Budinski might not be calling at my office anymore.

The door closed behind me. To my right the shadowy corridor stretched the length of the hotel. From somewhere down the hall came the sound of a boombox, the thump of a bass guitar, and Madonna moaning about Love.

I shivered and turned in the other direction.

# Chapter Fifteen
## A fern by any other name would smell as sweet

3:03 p.m.

The elevator rose to the main floor and stopped. The doors opened, then started to close again. I saw someone heading my way and reached over to lean on the Open button. The iron curtains parted to admit the barmaid from last night, Fern and her little red Bunny outfit.

With a tray of drinks balanced on her upturned hand, she came aboard and tucked herself in the corner by the controls. "Thanks, honey." Fern threw a quick professional smile in my direction. She bent her knees and reached down for button number TWO, taking, in passing, another sidelong glance at me and my electric-green outfit. The elevator lifted off, climbed half a floor, then groaned to a stop. The ceiling light went out and a small battery powered emergency light on a high shelf snapped on.

"Damn!" Fern insistently thumbed her number again and again. "You know, the thing's always getting stuck." She tried all the buttons, one through twenty, but nothing happened. "These junky old elevators just weren't designed for *hotel*traffic. Only meant for a nice quiet apartment building, you know. Give it a minute and it will start up again." She poked the Two button in the eye a couple more times, then gave up. Turning to me, she added, "That's what the dive used to be, an apartment."

"So I heard. Don't suppose it would do any good to poke around in that hole where the emergency button used to be?" I pointed to the hole in the panel.

"I seriously doubt it, honey. But I'll give it try." Rattling glasses and slopping liquor but miraculously spilling not a drop, Fern put her tray down on the floor below the control panel. She peeked into the hole, and then with the heel of her hand pushed the red knob beside it marked FIRE "Nah. I knew it wouldn't do much good, the phone neither." She picked up the instrument to show me the hole where the microphone should have been. "Hello!" she yelled into the earphone, then jammed the thing back into its cradle.

"Anyway, you know that boy Buddy doesn't have a clue how to fix something *complicated*like a phone or an elevator. Damn!" Fern punched all the numbered buttons again with her manicured thumb. "Someone should torch the dump for the insurance. Go for it! And wouldn't you know it? I'm on alone right now." Fern tapped her toe, the picture of impatience.

"You know, I shouldn't really be doing room service, but sure can't afford to pass up the tips. Slavery ain't dead yet, honey." She kicked off her red high heels and stood in her pantyhosed feet, wriggling her toes. "Without the tips, the job just ain't worth the trouble."

I peeled hair off my forehead. "Are the tips that good?"

Sizing me up, Fern's eyes bounced back and forth, from my electric-green tits to my fluorescent ass to the damp towel around my shoulders. Possibly our shared near-nakedness, the sisterhood of the scantily clad, made a difference. Or perhaps, just being marooned together made it happen. Whatever the reason, Fern began to open up to me, speaking woman to woman, so to speak.

"Tips? Sure. But y'all have to put on a bit of a show, you know. If y'all have some farmer showing off for his friends, act real sweet and he'll always tell you to 'Keep the change, sugar.' And you can usually soak the ones who are too shy to come down to the bar." She gave me a sly smile. "Some of those good old boys get their kicks having a babe in undies bring drinks to their bedrooms. You know, you can always spot them--the ones who think it's a big thrill--as soon as they open the door, you can just see their tongues hanging out."

Fern acted out the scene, flashing her teeth as she made her entrance.

"Y'all walk in real slow, show them your glutes when y'all put down the drinks, cock your hip and put out your hand. Then you slip their money between your 'mamms'--the old ones really like that--then get out fast." Fern moonwalked on the spot--a self-mocking performance.

Unlike some of the other hotel employees, Fern seemed to know she was acting a part. She played the role with conviction but obviously didn't take it too seriously. Drawing the towel around my shoulders, I asked. "Isn't it dangerous?"

Fern swatted the air with the flat of her hand. "Nah!" She ran her eyes over my figure. "Y'all could do it, girl. It's good money."

"And it's almost tax-free?"

 I watched Fern look me over. Perhaps, for a moment, she was measuring me against her stereotype of the tax inspector. Then she shrugged off my tax question. "Mind if I smoke?"

"Yes, I do."

Her hand poised over her waist, like a gunslinger's, the server turned slowly and gave me a Try and Stop Me look. Then Fern thumped her fist against the elevator door.

"If you really need one, I'll survive it."

"Why, thank you, girl." From out of a tiny pocket in the bib scwn into the front of her red corset, Fern pulled a cigarette and a lighter. She lit up, inhaled deeply, then blew a great cloud of smoke at the elevator ceiling.

Away from the gloom of the bar, Fern seemed just as remarkable. Like a Vogue model, her platinum-blonde, flattop hairdo was perfectly shaped, and her lips shone with a crimson cover-girl gloss, and her figure was the stuff of men's fantasies. Part fashion plate, part sex object; I figured my dad would call her, "all woman." No doubt about it, Fern definitely had style, a real walking, talking, living doll. Of course, the sisters would say this doll's style, from hairdo to high heels, was a blend of purely male designs. Still, she was incredibly good-looking.

More than anything else since our first meeting, Fern's eyes were what grabbed my attention. Deep blue and constantly moving, I could imagine them working the room downstairs, checking for the tip on the table, searching for the hand raised for a round of drinks or a hungry man. Catching myself staring, I covered up with the first question that popped into my head. "Are you an American?"

"American? Don't I wish." Fern rolled her eyes. "Whatever gave you that idea? I was born in Ontario, an army brat. The old man and old lady both died in an auto accident in Germany. After that an Air Force couple over there adopted me." Taking a quick drag on her smoke, she added, "When I was twelve the family got transferred back here. So I guess I'm a Canadian twice over. Tough eh?"

"You talk like an American."

"That's the kind of English I learned in Germany."

"Oh." I acknowledged my error with an apologetic nod. "Were your adoptive parents good people? You close to them?"

Fern studied the drift of her smoke. "She's fine, he was a pig."

I gave the air a little kick. "Have you worked here long?"

"Long enough. I'm a nurse, actually. Well, nearly a nurse." Fern shook her head in disgust. "Just have to finish a few courses at the University Hospital. Been trying to get them done for a couple of years now, but something always seems to come up. Y'all know what I mean?"

"Really. That must be tough, working and studying at the same time."

"Honey, you don't know the half of it." Fern braced her free hand on her hip and lifted the other one to her mouth. Closing her eyes, she dragged hard on the cigarette. The smoke floated slowly out of her nose and curled up through her hair towards the light in the ceiling.

"I'm kind of surprised to find a nurse who smokes."

"Find me a nursing job, honey, and I'll quit right now." Fern glared, daring me to continue my line of inquiry.

I held up my hands in surrender.

Neither of us said anything for a minute, then I asked, "Did you know Norman Water?"

Fern took another long drag on her cigarette. She blew a smoke ring and gazed at the hot tip of burning tobacco. "No. No, I didn't." Raising her eyes again, she looked straight at her inquisitor, before letting her gaze drift back towards the thin blue line of smoke curling around her fingers. "But, you know, they say he was very light."

"Light?"

Fern nodded sagely. "You know, like the beer."

"By the way, I'm Regina Colwell." The politician stuck out her hand.

The citizen nodded at it. "I know that, honey."

Taking back my hand, I rubbed the goose bumps off my arms. There seemed to be nothing more to say, so we waited in silence.

Without a sound, the elevator car suddenly dropped a few inches, and the two of us froze, but after a few seconds we looked up, laughed and relaxed. When the machine slipped down another foot, I grabbed Fern's arm for support. For a long moment, we stood like that, barely daring to move.

From the well below came a mechanical squeak, then the lights flickered on, and with a sudden lurch, the elevator started up again.

"Must have been a power failure." I released Fern from my grip.

"Yeah." Fern stepped into her high heels, threw her cigarette on the floor and crushed it under her shoe. I held the door, while she picked up her tray and exited onto the second floor. As I watched Fern tote her load of drinks down the hall, I couldn't help thinking how much my swimsuit resembled Fern's corset and how I would never, ever, have the guts to do her job. As they say around here, she was very good at what she does.

Manic Man, the tour group complainer, nipped aboard just ahead of the closing doors. He saluted me and pressed the button for the tenth floor. He peered at the controls for a minute, then seeing that someone had programmed stops at every floor, he gave me, my wet towel and my green fluorescent swimsuit a fierce look.

"Young lady, you look old enough to know better than to fool around on public conveyances. I've a good mind to report you."

For reasons that were not completely clear to me, I responded by clowning around--an understandable giddiness after being trapped in the elevator, I hoped. Perhaps I did it because the audience was American and couldn't vote. Or maybe Manic Man's face made me do it. Affecting my little girl voice, I said, "Pardonnez-moi, Monsieur. C'est le premier fois que je reste dans un hotel aussi grand."

Manic Man frowned and stuck out his jaw.

Close to giggles, I got off at the next stop. I pushed the Up button and waited for another car. When it arrived, I crowded in with some of Manic Man's fellow travellers. All of the travellers squeezed to the rear to avoid contact with my wet swimsuit. I stood with my back to them at the front of the car, making wet footprints onto the floor.

"Her hair's wet," one of the visitors whispered.

"Shush, Mary!" said her friend. "You almost got us in trouble already talking too loud about that drag queen in the dinner jacket."

At the seventh floor, I turned and waved good-bye to the tourists. It occurred to me that, if it were not for the hotel and its staff, I could be having a really good time.

# Chapter Sixteen
## Room for the day, if you can pay

Saturday, April 1

4:14 p.m.

In my room again, I locked the door and peeled the green layer off my pink skin. Inserting a hanger under the shoulder straps, I suspended the wet fluorescent thing from the curtain rail above the balcony window. It hung there limp, like a radioactive weed from outer space, a foreign flash of colour in a grey Canadian day.

Down below on the sidewalk, a handful of tiny humans moved here and there, bucking the squalls, the shopping bags on their arms whipping about like kites. The Saturday afternoon streets looked almost empty.

I inspected the room. The maids had invaded and put everything back in place just as if nobody had slept here last night or the night before that or on any night from the first moment of Greenwood's time. They'd readied the room for the next guest. Whether I stayed or moved on, it made no difference. I had no history here, and no future.

I found it impossible to relax in the room. It was a bit too much like staying in my father's new house, which resembled not at all the musty nest I'd fled on graduation. It would take a long time to turn Room 701 into my Home Sweet Home. I could not move the furniture around or decorate the walls, for these were not my things. They were, and would forever be, someone else's things, or nobody at all's.

Even the idea of wrinkling the bedspread made me slightly uneasy. I might put the chain on the door, but I still could never comfortably lie around in my underwear or relax in the bath, for fear that something awkward would happen. Bud might barge in with his mop, or Rose could charge in looking for a fight. Nor could I content myself sitting quietly, reading stories about the financial crisis on Prairies farms, or famine in Africa, while the mystery of the boy who died in 505 kept nagging at my brain.

Why not break a habit, Regina. Face your fears. Act creatively for a change. For once in your life, do absolutely nothing. Just wait and see what happens. Very deliberately, I lay back on the bed and stared up at the ceiling. But, no matter how hard I tried, I could not put my mind to rest. After five minutes I quit trying. I got up, dressed and brushed my hair.

Picking up the phone book, I leafed through the white pages. The book had several listings for Water, including a Norman Water Sr. I dialled the number, but a recording told me that it "was no longer in service." Information had no new number listed. I called long-distance information for Toronto. No Water, Norman, senior or junior, the operator said. Picking up the phone again, I bobbled the receiver in my hands for a minute, trying to decide whom to call next. Cradling the instrument on my shoulder, I dialled my storefront office.

Heather was prompt, answering on the first ring, turning down the radio with her free hand.

"How's it going down there?" To my ears the question sounded horribly inane, but after my last conversation with Heather I really didn't know how else to break the ice.

"Fine. Except that I do swear to get a good night's sleep tonight."

"Promises, promises." I admired my aide's abundance of social graces.

"It's going to catch up with me one day," Heather moaned. "The nuns did warn me."

"You've never worried about that before. You used to say you'd sleep when you retired," I said, as much to myself as to her.

Heather answered through a yawn. "Say a prayer for me then. I'm not sure I can wait that long."

"Any customers? Any messages?" Over the telephone line, I heard Heather shuffling papers on her desk.

"Business has been slow. A couple of unemployment insurance cases, and I've got one of your homeless people with me now. He really liked the story in today's paper, by the way."

"He did?" I asked, suddenly alert.

"Yes. He liked it so much he wants us to find a house for him."

"God, I hope you told him that people are lined up around the block just to get on the waiting list for public housing?" I twisted the telephone cord around my index finger.

"Surely. But he's after something a little more grand. He fancies one of those new high-rise condominiums you were talking about, preferably one overlooking the park."

"He does, does he? Did you tell him we do the art of the possible, not the impossible?"

"Would you like to talk to him?"

I paused, my finger in mid twist. "Is he a nut?"

"Not exactly, but he looks like a difficult case, and you did tell me to refer all difficult cases to you."

"Okay." I sat up straight on the edge of the bed ready for the Difficult Case.

"Hey, man, what's happening?"

"Moss? You bum! I thought it really was a homeless person." I untangled the cord from my finger, lifted my feet up onto the bedspread and propped myself against a fluffed-up pillow.

"You should take me more seriously, Reggie, for I am indeed a homeless person. Can't you see the headline? 'Evicted by Heartless Politician: Rejected Reporter Tells All.' Paragraph. "A celebrated city journalist found himself out on the street today, after a run-in with his landlord, MLA Regina Colwell. In public, Colwell champions the cause of the homeless, but when it comes to her private interests she's an unforgiving slum lord.' Do you like the lead? It needs work, but it's a great story."

Lifting my head, I massaged my neck. Moss might be joking, but I detected the hint of a threat in his jest. "You're not homeless. You're just another unrepentant baby boomer yearning for his lost youth, free love, open marriages and all that retro Sixties shit."

"You're a cruel woman, Regina Colwell."

"If I were really unkind, I'd say you are just another suburban male in search of some old-fashioned, recreational nookie."

"Wow. That is hitting below the belt."

Exasperated by the day's dealings with difficult people, I let my tongue lash out. "A yuppie bigamist, that's what you are: two cars, two homes, two wives. Eh?"

"Wow." Moss exhaled slowly. "Robyn and I just lived together, Regina. You know we weren't committed to anything serious." He paused a contrite moment before speaking again. "That crummy hotel must be really getting to you, eh?"

I rolled my head again, then let it drop back onto the pillow. "I'm fine. What have you been up to?"

I heard an explosion of fizz at the other end of the line as Moss opened a pop-top can in front of the mouthpiece.

"Me?" he asked. "I spent a lovely time out of the weather in the new underground malls connected to the downtown office towers. It has given me a new perspective on the future. Here's the way I see it. The developers are already preparing for global warming, the nuclear winter or both. In the interconnected malls, the underground parking garages, the automatic bank tellers and the mass-produced teriyaki pizzas, one can see the beginnings of a post-holocaust troglodyte culture. In a year or two it'll be possible to live, eat, sleep and work without ever seeing the light of day. You'll be able to travel for miles beneath the streets of the city and never need a car or even a coat. Parkas will become a thing of the past."

"Morlocks? H. G. Wells and The Time Machine. Right?"

"Right on." Moss took a noisy swig from his can. "Well, HG, I have seen the future, too, but unfortunately the architecture and the food are not for me. I ate lunch today at a place called Mac's Tacos. Another bad marriage of cuisines, I'm afraid. They should have called it 'Tacky Too.' Fasting may be tough, but fast food will be the death of us all. I've decided I like my food nice and slow, thank you."

"Sounds like a good policy."

"Say, do you reckon Norman Water could have been fasting?"

"No. I don't think he was the type."

"Then it's elementary, my dear Colwell. Fast food did him in."

"Can't be the whole story, but thanks for the thought anyway."

"That's cool. Hey, the news is not all bad. Today I saw a very old man with a hickey, so I know there's hope for me yet, man."

"So, you had fun. I, on the other hand, spent the morning wrestling with oxymorons."

"Like fast food?"

"Like business ethics, hospitality industry and friendly service."

"What you radicals used to call contradictions, eh?" Moss took another drink. "I guess you're really sold on that hotel, eh?"

"Definitely a No-Star rating in my book. And the management is full-moon crazy: Digger, Queenie, the whole bunch."

"Well, you know what they say in the hotel industry: It's a crazy business, and management is everything."

"I never heard that before, but, brother, I believe it." I stretched forward, touched my toes with my free hand, then swung my legs off the bed. "Speaking of management, can you do me a small favour?"

"Anything." Moss stifled a burp. "Within reason. What is it?"

I whipped the telephone cord round and round, like a skipping rope. "It's none of my business, but I'm curious. Greenwood claims he's a chartered accountant. So why did he let himself get appointed captain of this little Titanic? Why does he take on a strange bruiser like Queenie De Lis as his first mate? And what kind of work was Herb Kohl doing before he landed here? Lily White, too? Can you believe that name? The things parents do to their kids! Anyway, that dear, sweet little old lady is a short-change artist, and it may not be not a brand new line of work for her. Can you check the newspaper files for their names? Scandals, lawsuits, arrests, convictions: You know, the kind of muck the media loves to dig up."

"You mean dirt. We dig dirt; we rake muck. Sure, that won't take me long: Digger Greenwood, Herb Kohl, Queenie De Lis and Lily White. A spade forest, a spicy cabbage and two lilies; that should be easy enough to remember. If necessary, I'll pay a call on a fuzzy friend at the cop shop, too. But it will cost you."

I adjusted the phone in my hand. "What?"

"Dinner tonight?"

"I don't think I can leave here right now, Moss."

"Man, I thought you hated the place. But that's cool. Shall we eat at six? I have something to cover in that neighbourhood anyway. Your treat?"

"Okay. Dinner here at six, but no canoodling. Promise?"

"Don't even know the word. Is it a pasta dish?"

"Six." I laid the phone to rest.

# Chapter Seventeen
## Would you like your turndown bedded?

Saturday, April 1

5:34 p.m.

I steeled myself.  To crack the Norman Water case, I'd have to go another round with Rose, the hard-rock housekeeper.  I had time enough before dinner--if I could find her.  A big "if."

According to Lily, Rose and Norman had been lovers, although Rose herself had showed nothing but contempt for the young man--a nice contradiction that.  Norman didn't seem very loveable, and Rose could hardly be called loving.  Opposites were supposed to attract but not creatures from different planets.  As far as I could see, these two had nothing in common save their youth and their place of work.  Unless I was very wrong, Norman was not exactly Rose's kind of guy.  Norman and Rose Water, at the altar, promising to love, honour and obey?  No way.  What in heaven's name could Norman have seen in Rose?  What would she have found appealing about him?  Only the housekeeper could tell that tale.  Only she knew the truth about the relationship, and I felt an urgent need to know.

The elevator car struggled down to the lobby.  In search of the housekeeper's headquarters, I went past the manager's office, along the hall and down the stairs into the basement.  In the hotel, I noted, each job had its own private domain.  Every worker had a corner, a desk, a staff table, a laundry room or a broom closet.  Everyone had a base from which to make their sorties out into the wider workaday world of lobby, bar, restaurant, hallways and guest rooms.  All understood the boundaries of their occupational territories: private places and public spaces; separate worlds defined by walls and floors, doors and rules.

The chef had his kitchen, the clerk had her desk and the manager his office, but only the manager and his muscle could roam the property at will, private places as well as public spaces, in Digger Greenwood's dominion.

I thought back to my brief fling with juvenile delinquency. Private Property and Trespassers Beware signs had fascinated me back then. What a temptation they had presented to a teenager with time on her hands. With my friend Minny Miller, I'd climbed some razor-wire fences and broken into a couple of warehouses near the rail yards. We didn't steal or damage anything. The payoff was the excitement of doing something forbidden. One time though, I was rattling a door knob, when Miller suddenly swore and started running. I had no idea why she'd bolted but I chased her up the alley. When I caught up, Minny yelled, "God, Reggie, didn't you see the light go on in that building? We could have got caught!"

"No," I said and we laughed. But that cured me of B and Es.

Now that I had strayed from the public areas, I was not a guest anymore but a trespasser once again. It was a the same cheap thrill all over again but what's a vacation without a little adventure.

On the back stairs and in the basement, the hidden realm of the housekeepers and handymen, the building gave up any pretence of decoration, any illusion of comfort. Just as Greenwood's no-frills approach showed his indifference towards his customers, these surroundings reflected exactly the hotel's attitude towards its employees, the women and men who kept the place clean, fed and watered. These walls had never felt paint. No carpet had ever touched the floors. The air smelled of Lysol, mildew and dust. It was a cold hard place and I loved its brutish charm.

I stepped into the corridor. Here, the shape of things in Greenwood's moneymaking machine was all too plain. The structure overhead consisted simply of stacks of concrete boxes. Little boxes fitted within bigger and bigger boxes until they finally filled up one great big box. Concrete walls and concrete floors had been cemented into concrete rooms, one on top of another until the land beneath could take no more. Here was architecture I could comprehend. Every day people put a little money into each of the boxes and, after a time, it all added up to big money.

Proceeding cautiously, like a blind person, I reached out my hands, feeling my way along the corridor. With my fingertips, I explored the coarse concrete walls. With the toes of my Docs, I tentatively stepped on the cracks in the floor. Only the occasional naked forty-watt bulb provided any relief from the black shadows and the rough grey walls. Most of the light sockets sat empty. Others contained bulbs that were burned out, or turned out, which, I could not tell.

My eyes tracked up the dimpled walls to the ceiling beams. Between the joists, I saw half a dozen shiny, coloured cylinders running side by side down the length of the corridor. These, I assumed, were the pipes and ducts taking the heat and water and light hither and yon. Here were red pipes, orange pipes, blue pipes, green pipes and grey pipes. Here lay the hotel's intestines, arteries and veins, the guts of the machine, exposed like the innards of a wounded robot in a Hollywood fantasy, but I saw no movie. This represented hard reality, the really basic stuff: hot water, cold water, waste water, fresh air, fuel oil, natural gas, electricity.

I tried to crack the code. Was the blue pipe for cold water and the red for hot? Was the orange one for oil? And the brown one destined for the sewer? Perhaps the green one contained something else? Money, maybe?

I strained my eyes, studying the brightly coloured pipes. If this was a movie and I was the heroic environmental avenger, I would be providing a running commentary through a nifty headset back to my base. My analysis would describe my findings: fresh water and fossil fuels in; waste water and hot air out to the great beyond. A river dammed and the air polluted for the sake of a wired city, TV sets and burned-out forty-watt bulbs. I would tell my green comrades of the weight I felt dragging in my guts. Would the dinosaurs have died in peace, if they'd known their bones would come to this? Hearing me, my colleagues would urge me past the next obstacle.

And I would lift my head and put my best foot forward. As I passed by a metal door marked Mechanical Room, an electric pump started up inside, momentarily dimming the lights, and my heart skipped a beat. In the movie, I would stop and stand perfectly still. Through the soles of my shoes, I'd feel the floor throb, as the huge complex of concrete boxes, the money machine, sucked the life out of the earth.

Suddenly, a loud noise brought me back to reality.

From down the hall came the sound of rap music played at full volume. In the same vicinity an unbalanced washer started to madly hump a dryer. Bang, bang, squeak, squeak, thump, thump. I followed the sound towards a wedge of fluorescent light that spilled into the corridor from an open door. Quietly, I crept up to the light.

In the middle of the laundry room, oblivious to the racket, stood Rose, boombox between her feet, her eyes fixed on the window of an industrial dryer, as sheets and towels tumbled over and over and over inside. I waited for Rose to notice my arrival, but she remained rooted to the spot, her back to the door.

I coughed, but the housekeeper did not respond. I called Rose's name, but the woman still did not move. Only when I shouted over the din, did Rose turn around and then very slowly, as if she'd known she had company all along but couldn't be bothered to entertain right now.

I repeated her name, but Rose just looked right through me, as if on the trip down the dark corridor, I had become completely invisible. I appealed to Rose with my hands, but the housekeeper just stood stiff like a robot, her eyes giving me the Look, while the boombox screamed, "Kill the motherfucking motherfuckers" and the unbalanced washer hammered the dryer sideways.

After five seconds of this, I knew the sting of rejection; after ten, I felt only embarrassment. Another few seconds and I could stand it no more. Moving around Rose, I lifted the lid to the washer, waited for the agitator to stop, and reached in to balance the load. With Rose glaring at me, I backed out of the room and followed the coloured pipes to the concrete stairs, flicking off switches along the way, killing the naked lights, blacking out the basement corridor completely, leaving the bare walls and the hard floors and the marked doors and Greenwood's bloody moneymaking machines to their own devices.

At the foot of the stairs I paused by a garbage dumpster to look at the soiled blanket in the corner where someone must have been sleeping. I wondered wonder how long it would take them to connect Greenwood's Apartment Hotel to Moss's underground city.

# Chapter Eighteen
## Fast food, that's what you are

Saturday, April 1

6:01 p.m.

I closed the door, unplugged the radio and TV, and turned down the thermostat. I splashed cold water on my face and ran a brush through my hair. The phone rang. Picking it up, I whispered, "Hello," and sat down on the bed. Listening hard, I could hear breathing on the other end. Male or female, I could not tell.

"Who is it?" I demanded and the person at the other end hung up. Reaching down behind the bedside table, I unplugged the phone from the wall. Hanging the Do Not Disturb sign on the outside door knob, I crept down the hall and hiked down the back stairs to the lobby.

I picked up the pay phone and called the parental unit. "Dad, how are you?

"Fine. The old ticker is still ticking."

"Good. I've been thinking about what you said about Norman Water. You said he was brilliant at mathematics. Right? Can you tell me anything more about him than that."

"Not yet. I've been meaning to phone Mrs. Kite and I'll do that tonight, if you like."

"Thanks, Dad. I'd really appreciate that. Can you call me back at this number?" I gave him the hotel phone number and signed off.

Checking around, I saw Greenwood breaking in a new desk clerk, an angular youth with an earring and a stiff white shirt two sizes too big for him. I nodded at the manager, but he turned his head, suddenly finding something of interest on the cash register tape. Apart from Fern, Manic Man, and the day shift from the restaurant, the bar was practically empty.

The restaurant's lights were dimmed for the evening trade but the place was empty and, in there, I would nobody to talk with. After my initial encounter with Queenie, I had no wish to loiter in the lobby at night, and the bar looked uninviting. I didn't particularly want another elevator ride right now, I did not need to go back to my room and I'd seen more than enough of the basement. That left the restaurant. What the hell, I thought. You only live once, eh?

I examined the dining room--no more than the coffee shop disguised by dimmed lights and inflated prices. Seeing no staff around, I took a menu and seated myself where I could see the door. I noticed they had covered up the Arborite tops with tablecloths and camouflaged the cash desk with a salad bar.

The name on the menu was La Fin Diner. In Gothic type, the evening version listed all the items in French. Yet a close look at the list showed nothing but the standard meat-and-potato fare. The menu deviated from the sacred cow only for the day's special, Les Fruits de la Mer. The small print beneath the offering made it plain that the "*fruit*" in question was a combination plate featuring lobster from the East Coast and crab from the West, both no doubt deep frozen, although the menu didn't admit that.

Under a plastic clip marked Soupe du Jour, someone had stuck a hand-written slip of paper that said Vichyssoise. Kohl the old cosmopolitan had spelled the word correctly. Transcontinental crustaceans and cold spuds. I cast my eyes over the greens by the cash register, but even under the dim light the salad looked sadly limp.

A group of elderly tourists came in. They sat nearby and talked about their melanomas and their angioplasties. They compared hospitals and specialists, medical technologies and drug therapies. And, with a hoisting and a clinking of glasses, they toasted each other's good health.

"I think you must be used to eating good food," I overheard a dark, tanned one say.

"Do your girlfriends still eat a big noonday meal in Oregon, I mean Northern California?" asked a woman with facial skin stretched back to her ears.

"Women talk about their 'girlfriends,' but men never say anything about their 'boyfriends,'" said a third tourist.

They seemed to be having a good time, moving about, feeling alive. Foreign travel seemed to agree with them. I, on the other hand, felt deeply unsettled. Defeated by Rose and frustrated by the day, I also felt guilty about skipping my regular Saturday-morning office duties. An old stain on the tablecloth reminded me that I hadn't even done my laundry or cleaned my apartment this weekend. I'd read no book and written no letters. Nor had I figured out what happened to Norman Water.

What a strange boy. He'd drifted into the building, got in over his head, then buried himself in his room. Along the way, he'd managed to work his way down the ladder, one rung at a time, doing increasingly menial jobs and sinking deeper and deeper into debt. Yet he seemed to have made no real attempt to leave. Most people would have run like a thief from his situation. Certainly, I believed that's what I would have done at Norman's age. Straight home to Papa. Perhaps he had no place to go or some insanely good reason for staying put.

By all accounts, he had been an ineffectual lad, expressing himself forcefully only through his practical jokes. But even the pranks made sense only as a way of fighting back. Some of Norman's tricks clearly had some purpose in that they avenged some wrong he'd suffered, or imagined he'd suffered. For others, there seemed no motive. If I could establish the root cause of these incidents, would things become clearer?

Norman's personality must have seemed so unimposing that everyone saw him differently. He angered Greenwood, amused Kohl, embarrassed Lily, disgusted Rose and fascinated Bud.

Sometimes he seemed just like an echo chamber for much stronger characters.

Mainly, he was a watcher and a listener, one of those quiet types who always surprised everyone when they did something remarkable enough to reveal their secret life. I wondered if he'd seen or heard something that got him into trouble and led to his death. So far, I'd seen no sign of the brilliant high school student.

It just didn't seem possible the he was so "lite" that he just drifted into his room and quietly melted away, all memories of him being washed away almost overnight. Tracing the contours of the stain with the point of my butter knife, I realized that I had many questions and few answers.

Looking up, I saw Queenie leading Moss towards my table and tensed involuntarily at the sight of the dinner-jacketed bouncer. The response, it pleased me to note, was mutual. Queenie stopped yards short of my table and waved her customer onward.

Moss glanced back at Queenie. "Is she or isn't she?"

"What?"

"A drag king? A very masculine woman?" Moss sat down, slightly breathless. He'd put on a clean shirt, and a woven wool tie to go with his corduroy suit.

I shrugged at Queenie's retreating back. "You're wearing a tie, Moss."

He touched the knot, lifting his chin and stretching his neck. "Yes. I've been thinking about what you said on the subject of uniforms. Now, I wonder: Is the necktie a harness or a noose? What do you think?"

"My guess is that it began life as a bib. Take it off if you want."

"You don't think the maitresse de maison will be offended?"

"Fat chance. That's the assistant manager and chief bouncer--the one I told you about. Queenie De Lis."

"Is it really?" Moss craned around for another look at the woman.

"What kept you? I've been cooling my heels for half an hour."

"I hope you didn't get cold feet."

I gave Moss a gentle kick under the table.

"Sorry I'm late, but I had to cover a speech by your chum, Dandy Lyon, before coming here. Unfortunately they always run late at the legion hall."

"What was the speech about?"

"The Business of Government is Business, I think. My mind kept wandering, and I may have missed something."

"Boring, huh?"

"The thing is, Lyon talks fast but only half as fast as most people think, and the chatter at my table sounded at least as interesting as his speech. Something about the mayor and some land transaction. So, I lent one ear to Lyon and the other to the table talk."

"Did you find out anything?"

Moss scratched his beard. "From the legionnaires?"

"No, from your files. And the cops."

"Sure," he said, with a silencing finger to his lips. "But you have to feed me first. Let's order. I'm starving."

Queenie crept up on us, her pumps squeaking on the floor.

I decided to strike first. "Quel surprise! I didn't knew you worked as a waiter as well as a manager. Very democratic. I'm impressed."

"Look. I don't fancy this any more than you do, but the dinner waiter failed to show for his shift." The lurking brute touched her bow tie. "Have you decided?" she demanded, her eyes fixed on the order pad.

I ordered the soup and a salad.

"Do you have any fish?" Moss asked.

"Lobster," Queenie replied with a regal smile.

"How about something local?"

Queenie turned up her nose. "From around here? You must be joking?"

"Do you have any lake trout?"

"No."

"Sucker?"

Queenie's eyebrows closed like blinds over her eyes. She shook her head, stiffly.

After careful deliberation, Moss chose Le Boeuf au Jus. Queenie recommended an Okanagan red to go with it, but Moss wanted beer. Feeling slightly parched myself, I ordered some ice water. The paperwork done, Queenie breezed off in a cloud of Brut.

"The body beautiful, the mind ugly."

"Rambo," Moss added.

"Rambelle is more like it."

We both sniggered.

Queenie returned in a few seconds. "How did you want your beef."

Moss looked up. "Rare. Didn't I mention that."

Queenie sniffed. "Possibly. I did not write it down"

While we waited for our meal, more tourists came in to eat. From political habit, I nodded greetings. "I wonder why they come here?"

"I expect they've already been everywhere else."

"But why here?"

"Beats me. Fishing, swimming, boating; the usual tourist thing."

"I guess."

"That's it, you see. They want our water. "

I nodded. "Blue gold. Wasn't that what some newspaper called Canada's water?"

Moss smiled. "Man, you got that right. I saw it in the *National Post*. Did you ever hear about NAWAPA?"

"Is that an aboriginal name?"

"Not quite. The North American Water and Power Alliance was a wild scheme to construct a series of huge dams to control the Yukon, Peace and Liard rivers and divert the water into a fresh water canal running from the Canadian North to the American states. "

"That cannot be happening."

"Not yet but just you wait and see."

"People would fight it."

"You heard about Cochabamba?"

"That's the Bolivian city where the people protested the privatization of their local water?"

"Right. This was a pretty big deal. In 1998, the World Bank forced Cochabamba to privatize its water system in order to get a loan to rebuild their utility. A subsidiary of the American multinational Bechtel grabbed it up, and then without having invested a penny, the new owner doubled the water rates. For the poor there, water was now costing as much as food, and many were cut off. Then the World Bank got the Bolivian government to charge market rates to peasants farmers gathering rain water on their own lands. People were angry; a poll showed that 90% wanted Bechtel out, thousands marched on Cochabamba and the government declared martial law.

Six protestors died. Then Bechtel turned tail, took their money and ran."

"That's a happy ending, I suppose." I toasted Moss with my water glass. "But I wonder what will happen next."

"Stay tuned."

"We never seem to think things through until they're too late. You'll say it is way too pinko of me, but municipal sewer and water systems delivering clean healthy  drinking water to everyone at minimal cost are one of the great achievements of our civilization."

"Cochabamba was a small victory, but the water wars will continue. The World Bank says there's a trillion dollar market out there and the potential profits are enormous."

I looked at Moss. "I don't see much about this in your newspaper."

Moss bowed his head. "I only write the stories.  It's the editors who decide whether to run them. "

"You know my view: Privatization is theft of public property."

"Maybe, but it's worse than that.  Water's not just the life blood of our provincial economy, water is life itself. It's common inheritance, a public trust and the biggest environmental issue of all. Water is a human right, not a commodity."

"Moss, I've never seen you so heated before.  This is much more exciting than when you're hustling me."

My friend leapt at the chance to stop being so earnest. "Give me a chance and I'll show you just how passionate I can be."

"It's okay. I believe you.  But you don't really want me, do you?"

"You have no idea."

"Really?"

"Really."

I didn't really believe Moss, so I changed the subject. "Anyway, I guess Minister Lyon is right: government is a business and business is going to do everything it can to get government out of the water business."

"You can bet on it." Moss picked at a piece of bread. "Speaking of the water business, I wonder how your boy Norman Water would have voted?"

I looked down. "He'd have been a non voter, I expect."

"So, why do you think he had your name on his hand?"

"He was going to call me, of course."

"Why didn't he, then?"

"Maybe he couldn't for some reason, I don't know."

Moss cast a glance in Queenie's direction. "Is she really number two in here?"

"Greenwood's king of the castle. Next come Queenie and Kohl. Until today, I would have put Lily next, although I don't know about that anymore. Then it would be Holly, Fern and Rose, and the other minimum wage staff, down to Bud at the bottom. Bud does repairs and is mildly retarded; he's a constituent of mine."

"So he's part of you?" Moss deadpanned.

"I suppose so." My mind spun back to the day's encounters with constituent Bud.

"Where did Norman fit in?"

"I guess he eventually fell right off the charts."

Our food came. Queenie dropped the plates on the table and rushed off.

"She might be wearing a dinner jacket, but the service is strictly lunch counter," Moss observed.

I picked up my soup spoon. "How did your foray into the world of law enforcement go? What did you find out?"

"I spent a few minutes with some fuzzy buddies from the old police beat days, but they wouldn't tell me much. So I ran back to the office to poke around in the morgue."

"The morgue?"

"The newspaper's archives."

"So. What did you find?"

"According to *National Geographic*, every day the average American uses 87 gallons of water for flushing, 32 for showers, laundry and dish washing, but only two for drinking and cooking."

"What else?"

"Everyone has a secret. Everyone is a criminal." Moss smiled with his eyes.

"Kafka, right?"

"Patience, man." Moss pulled out his notebook and looked around quickly. "First, neither the rag nor the cops have a thing on Kohl. But get this. Tonight, the University Hospital admitted a Miss Lily White. She's in intensive care. A neighbour found her--in the garage, with her car running."

I let my spoon slide into the soup.

"That's not all. Our waiter Queenie is a very naughty lady. She has a record for assault: four arrests and two convictions. Apparently, at her previous job she attacked a customer in a buffet queue because the man took too much roast beef. The police have reason to believe, as they say, that she's into other stuff as well, exactly what, they wouldn't specify."

"She's scum." I fished around for my spoon. After wiping off the handle with a corner of the table cloth, I spooned up a couple of mouthfuls.

"Dregs, I think. Scum at the top, dregs at the bottom. Lyon is scum."

I conceded the point with a little bow. "What about Greenwood? He's smart and cute but a real dink, as far as I'm concerned."

Moss flipped a page in his book. "Greenwood? He's not exactly clean either. He has never been convicted of anything but there was a commercial fraud investigation into the accounting firm where he worked--and he left their employ not long afterwards."

"That's interesting."

"Both of these creeps have to behave themselves. Neither is a citizen, only a landed immigrant. If they go down for something serious, they could be deported."

I tentatively dipped my spoon in the soup again. "They're pathetic, both as hoteliers and as crooks."

"Hey. There's nothing magic about the hotel business," Moss put in. "A hotel exists to make money. If they could make a buck without rooms or restaurants or workers, they'd do it. If they can't make any real money, they might as well burn it down and collect the insurance."

"Don't even hint at that--not while I'm kipping here."

"I take it all back. But we're not coming here on our honeymoon."

"You'll just have to take Robyn then." I tried to stay light-hearted. "But what about service? Even low-rent places are supposed to be part of the so-called service industry, aren't they?"

"You want service nowadays, you have to pay for it. The kinds of waiters who bow and scrape convincingly earn more than both of us put together. But doesn't that kind of service seem to belong to a class system that's supposedly long gone?"

"Greenwood would probably buy that, but I don't believe it for a minute. Precious few servers make more than you do, Moss, even if they perform like superstars. Why does service have to involve servility, anyway?  Give me one good reason why we can't serve each other?  Eh?"

Moss chewed, slowly.

"The soup tastes funny."

"What do you expect from cold potatoes."

I gave up on the soup.  "Everybody in the place seems to hate working here, and they all do their work so badly.  Like Lily, they're all nervous, suspicious or angry.  No happy faces at all.  Not even Queenie, and she might be one server who really does earn more than you or me--but not from waiting tables."

"Sure, but it's better here than in the communist countries.  I went to Cuba on holiday once.  You should see their beach bars.  They have six people doing the work of one.  Even I couldn't bear to watch them trying to act busy.  Too much like the Legislature.  You know what I mean.  You have one politician up on his feet whoring after a headline, while the rest of you sit around waiting your turn.  Anyway, your man Castro may have full employment, but he's got zero efficiency."

"My man?  I never even met the guy.  As you can see, they don't have much efficiency in here either.  What this place needs is a hard-assed union."  I pushed away the soup bowl.

"It might, but you couldn't organize the place.  The owners would fire the employees, fold the company or flip the property before the union got to first base."

"If that didn't work, they'd buy off the ringleaders."

"Sure, they'd all be made assistant managers."

I adjusted the position of the soup bowl until it covered the stain on the tablecloth.  "I've heard of crippling debt, but do you think it can it be a killer?"

"Sure, just ask Russia."

"When debt slaves fight back, do they have to die?"

"Master Water?"

"Norman was a bit of practical joker."

"In my experience the practical joker is usually someone trying to play God--you know, the invisible hand of humiliation.  The god Water feeds all living things and rests in the low places that humans avoid."

"Norman didn't seem very godlike.  Did the police know anything about him?"

"I did ask, but no.  They're waiting for the pathologist's report."

I lifted my fork and poked at my salad.  "I can't stop thinking about that kid sitting all alone for weeks on end in front of a TV set."

"Water does not run uphill, Reggie."

"In plants, it does."

"Whatever.  You can't change history.  People aren't going to trash their home-entertainment centres until something better comes along.  TV is nice.  It has a soft, warm glow that is very comforting to us lonely people.  It doesn't make us think or talk.  We don't have to do anything but sit and watch and listen."

"I watch the news, Moss, and there's only one perspective on the airwaves, and that's the American one.  I mean how am I supposed to know what the Russians think? Or the Chinese."

"Regina, this is not an constituency rally."

Shoving my salad plate to one side, I pleaded with Moss, "Am I wrong, or are people losing their appetite for life?  People are forgetting how to act politically.  Nobody's out there arguing for the greater good anymore.  We let second-rate actors live life for us, letting them do all the heroic and wonderful things while we sit and watch their adventures."

Moss grunted amiably. "You're a snob, Reggie, an old fashioned snob. TV is better entertainment than a boring wife, a nagging husband or squabbling children. It doesn't solve anything, but it's better than drugs or guns, much better."

"How can you be so sure about that, Moss? Everything comes to us in living colour and stereo sound. It's all sex and violence and noise. Wham, bam, screw you, ma'am. It's so overdone, so obviously inflated."

"Stop." Moss held up his hand. "You'll turn me into a Tory, if you keep it up. Are you sure TV's not getting a bum rap? What you say about TV could also be said of politics, couldn't it?"

"Sure, and I don't just mean Bush and Gore. That's how one gets elected to national office nowadays. Capped teeth, a sexy slogan and a batch of buzz words blended by pollsters into advertising blitzes."

"Not in your case. You've branded yourself as a lippy punk, and the media plays along."

"Also intelligent."

"And cute."

"Cute?"

"Repetition is the essence of political communication, surely. Television was made for politics. It's very democratic. Everyone watches the same programs, sees the same faces, hears the same songs, again and again."

"No, Moss! It's completely dictatorial. The advertisers talk, we listen. One-way communication. You can't talk back."

I watched Moss waiting for me to finish. He wasn't listening exactly. He had simply paused for a yellow light. When I stopped, it would be his turn to talk.

"Regina, you think everything is political..."

"I do.  That's true."

" . . . An ongoing partisan debate."

"So?"

"What you won't admit is that most of the time most people just don't care.  Our kind of democracy depends on their apathy."

"I care."

I felt tears welling up in my eyes.  "I try so effing hard, but nothing I do seems to matter.  Look at Norman Water.  He needed my help, and I didn't even know he was here.  I'm a member of the provincial Legislature--the youngest woman ever elected--but sometimes I feel totally powerless."

"Everybody knows you care, Regina.  I was at your nomination meeting.  Remember.  The party members all knew you'd ditched the nose ring and the punked up hairdo on the way to the meeting but they chose you because you were exciting.  Unlike the old war-horse running for the nomination, you had energy and style and commitment...."

"And they thought I'd lose the seat."

"They thought you'd lose the seat, but go down fighting, and that's what they wanted this abrasive, hyper-political chick to do for them.  But you did it.  You won, not by much but you won.  Some people love you, others hate you.  But no one ignores you."

"The Tories hate me.  Lyon even threatened to throw me out of the legislature."

"You piss them off but they don't hate you.  You remind them of their troublesome daughters.  Of course, they'll try to defeat you.  That's to be expected.  If you want to do politics, you're going to have to fight, and you know it."

 I put down my fork and rubbed my eyelids.  "I'm sorry, Moss.  Let's change the subject."

"Okay." Moss swallowed the last of his beef. "I'll tell you a joke. A wealthy and beautiful woman, an heiress, calls her butler into her bedroom. 'Take off my dress, Jones.... Now my slip...Undo my bra, Jones....Now my panties....And Jones, don't let me catch you wearing my clothes again!'"

I stifled a laugh. My body started to shake. I hid my face in my hands.

"What's up, man? Did I say something wrong?

"Moss, I caught Lily stealing from me today. That's why she did it, that thing in her garage."

"Oh, man." Moss came and put his arm around my shoulders.

I paid the bill, counting out the cash onto the table, bowing my head so that my hair hid my tearstained face. Queenie stood by, her eyes pin balling from customer to cash, from cash to customer, until all the money was all on the table. "Should we leave a tip?" I tried to smile through my hair. "Tipping is a remnant of feudalism," I said in a shaky voice. "What do you say? Ten per cent?"

"Make it fifteen per cent or she'll tear our heads off," Moss hissed.

Leaving the restaurant, I lifted my head and spotted Rose and Kohl in heated conversation over by the kitchen door. I could not hear what the two of them were talking about because they broke off the conversation as soon as they saw me coming their way. The cook handed something to the housekeeper, then, with a cheery wave at me, he retreated into his kitchen.

"That's Rose. And Kohl."

"What was that he handed her?"

"It looked like a bag of grass to me."

"Me too."

For a while, we stood in the lobby and watched a gentle rainfall.

"I like the rain," Moss said.

I put my hand on his arm. "It's time for you to move on, Moss."

"I'm lonely."

"We're all lonely, Moss."

"Oh," he said, suddenly wordless.

In the silence, my mind wandered off to the suicidal desk clerk and the boy from Room 505.

Moss touched my cheek.

My eyes came back into focus. "I'm sorry Moss, but I'm not in the mood for foreplay. Some truly shitty things happened here in the last couple of days. I may have had something to do with them, and it's driving me slightly crazy."

Moss put his hands on my shoulders, and we stood like that while Madonna serenaded us from a ceiling speaker. Moss's jacket had a familiar, musty scent. I breathed it in and clung to the corduroy. I felt fine standing like that with my friend, but as soon as I closed my eyes, pictures of Lily and the boy in the bath popped into my head. I blinked and twisted my head to one side.

"Would you like a massage?"

"No, thanks. I'm just tired."

"Can I kiss you goodnight?"

I looked at the gentle eyes, the soft pink lips and the frame of curly hair around the boyish face. "Why?"

"I'm going to look at a place on Monday."

"We'll shake on it." I offered my hand. "Now, let's call it a day. Okay?"

Moss shook my hand. "Okay. It's a day."

I watched Moss go off into the night, then stopped at the front desk. "Any messages for me? My name is Regina Colwell and I'm in Room 701."

The kid behind the counter opened a drawer and looked into a folder. "Just one."

I took the message slip. "Thank you."

"No problem."

"Your father called. He said: I phoned Mrs. Kite. She says Norman was not exactly brilliant but he had a phenomenal memory--what some people call photographic. He was particularly quick at arithmetic and, at a glance, he could remember long rows of numbers and recreate the list with perfect recall. He was also an acutely sensitive boy who never forgot or forgave a slight."

"Can you read my writing?"

"No problem."

I got myself onto the elevator. "Beam me up, Scotty." My body and mind moved and seconded a motion to adjourn.

# Chapter Nineteen
## Money = power = sex = love; Love is money

Saturday, April 1

7:57 p.m.

Back at 701, a cleaning cart blocked my doorway. I was about to push it out of the way when I noticed a little sleigh bell tied to the rubber grip on the handle. With one hand held onto the clapper of the bell, I gently pulled the cart a few feet down the hall.

I softly insinuated my room key into the lock. With the key in one hand and the handle in the other, I eased open the door and caught the housekeeper going through the pockets of my leather jacket. Rose froze on the spot, the guilty hand in mid-air. Crumpled in her fist was a wad of bank notes.

I lifted my leather jacket off the closet hanger. Without taking my eyes off Rose, I dipped into the pocket and pulled out my wallet. I flipped it open and felt inside the billfold. My cash was gone, all gone. "If you're going to be a thieving housekeeper, Rose It's not smart to take all the money."

Rose said nothing.

"Give it back." I put out my hand.

The housekeeper retreated a step. "It's not your money."

"Whose is it, then?"

"My tip."

"That's a big tip."

Rose nodded, once.

"Let me tell you something, Rose. You're not the only thief about the house. I've already been ripped off once today. I like to think of myself as a decent, forgiving person, but I'm not a complete mark. Nobody is going to make a fool of me twice in twenty-four hours. Not if I can help it. Take a good look at those bills in your hand. In the top left hand corner I think you'll find my initials and a number. That's enough to nail you for jail time."

Rose looked, peeling the corners back, one by one.

"That's right. They're on every one."

The housekeeper started for the door, but I blocked her exit, so Rose turned and retreated towards the balcony door. She stood by the glass door clutching the money and staring out at the rain.

"Rose?"

Rose turned slowly and came towards the bed, tears rolling down her cheeks. I reached for her, and the girl lost it.

"Leave me alone," Rose shrieked. "Leave me alone! You rich bitch. You effing stuck-up bitch, you." Her arms flailed in front of her as if she were warding off a swarm of enemies. The money flew out of her hand and fluttered down onto the carpet. Her shouts turned to wails, her eyes bulged and her face grew flushed. Then she started to shake her head violently as if trying to free herself of the demons inside.

I sat down on the edge of the bed. After a moment Rose did the same, her lips shaking as she tried to hold back her tears. I reached out and gently took her hand. "Are you in some kind of trouble?"

The girl nodded, twice.

"Pregnant?"

She nodded again.

"When are you due?" I asked.

"Fall."

"You need some help looking after the baby?"

Swallowing a mouthful of air, Rose shook her head. "I already got two kid."

"Do they stay with you?"

"My mom."

"Is Norman the father?"

Rose shrugged.

"Did you love him?"

Rose screwed up her face and shrugged again. "I figure if I did it with him, I can shack up with him, but he threw my clothes and stuff out the window. So I took his shirt, his short and suit and walked."

"Why did he do that?"

"I dunno."

"There must have been a reason."

"He said I scammed his stuff for drugs."

"What stuff?"

"He had big-screen TV, cost twenty-two-hundred buck, a seventeen-hundred-dollar CD player, video games. That kind of stuff."

"How could he afford all those things?"

"Credit card. See something on TV, phone in his number and then it comes. Just like that."

"But that didn't last long, did it? He was over his limit in no time. They repossessed the TV, didn't they? You didn't take it? Did you, Rose?"

"Nah. But, I did boost his CDs when I needed the bread."

"Did you buy drugs with Norman's credit card?"

Rose gave me The Look. "You can't score pot on credit."

"But you sold some of his things to get marijuana?"

Rose nodded.

I got up and walked slowly over to balcony door. I turned the handle, but the door was locked. "Did you ever meet his parents?"

"No."

Twisting the lock upwards, I opened the sliding-glass door to let in some humid night air. "They might help with the baby."

"They're long gone. They split the blanket. His dad went east. His mom had a breakdown. She went with her sis in California."

I took a breath of fresh air, then locked the balcony door. "Does he have other family here? Any relatives or friends of the family?"

"No. They only here one year."

"Where did the Waters come from?"

"I dunno."

Facing Rose again, I asked, "What happened to Norman?"

"Dunno."

"So, tell me if I've got this right? In July, Norman checked into the hotel with his credit card, but he soon reached his limit. So then he got a job on the front desk. That would be in September sometime. In October, he lost the desk job and went to work in the kitchen, but by November he ended up doing repairs."

"Repairs?"

"A handyman, right?"

"Right."

"That should have been in November, by my reckoning?"

"Yeah."

"When did you start?"

"When they went hotel, last summer. August, I guess."

"After Norman moved in?"

"Yes."

"And you started living with him when?"

Rose chewed her lip, thinking. "December."

"When did he get his eviction notice?"

"In December, right after I move in."

I fetched Rose some toilet paper from the roll in the bathroom, "Tell me, do you get paid more or less than a handyman or dishwasher?"

"We all get minimum wage, plus tips. Desk clerk get more 'cause they don't get much tip."

"So in the end Norman earned no more than you?"

"I guess. But we all thought he was loaded."

"Why?" I handed Rose the wad of toilet paper.

Rose blew her nose. "Well, he had a room here. And all that stuff."

"Is that why you wanted to move in with him?"

"I guess. My kid got problems, and my mom bitch all the time."

"What happened after Norman lost his job?" I asked.

"What you mean?"

"Did he get mad?"

"He don't shout like a white man. He just pay them back."

"How?"

Remembering, Rose smiled. "He mix up all names on laundry bag so men get women stuff, big people get small one, like that."

"Did he stone the mayor's prayer breakfast?"

Rose gave a throaty chuckle. "Oh, yeah. He drop acid in orange juice."

"Why did he do that?"

"He mad at those guy. And Herb."

Raising my eyebrows expectantly, I invited Rose to continue.

The maid bit at a hangnail. "Them holy rollers see me eating at staff table and bitch about it. They said I listen in on meeting. I told Herb I don't give a shit about white man meeting, but Herb kick me out anyways."

Recalling Rose's furtive exchange with Herb in the restaurant downstairs earlier that evening, I asked, "Kohl sells you drugs?"

"I told that guy you see us. But he said, 'she's cool.'"

"Great! The only one here who thinks I'm cool is a dealer. Did Greenwood know you stayed in Norman's room?"

With the back of her hand, Rose wiped her nose. "Guess so. Norman let all kinds of street kids crash for the night."

"Did Greenwood care about that kind of thing?"

"Not if you pay rent."

"But Norman didn't?

"Didn't what?"

"Pay the rent."

"No."

"Why didn't they evict him?"

"They want him out.  They try everything to make him pay, but he don't, so they gave him notice.  They about had him treed when something happen, and they stop trying.  So they just keep him here 'til he pay them."

"Something happened?  What happened?"

"I dunno."

"But Digger and Queenie stopped harassing him, right?"

"Yeah."

"When did you last see Norman?"

"Maybe one month ago.  I dunno."

"You didn't clean his room?"

"We don't do apartment."

"No, of course, you don't.  Did he talk to you when you saw him last?"

"Nobody could talk to him no more."

"Did anyone try?'

"Nah."

"Why not?"

"No money left.  Nothing nobody could do for him no more."  Rose scratched the tattoo on her arm.

"Nobody called the welfare office."

"Guess not."

Silent, Rose sat, staring at her boots.

I looked at the bad painting in the cheap frame on the far wall and tried to guess the odds of this young woman ever getting control of her life--hopelessly alienated, dysfunctional family, substance abuse. As a legislator I could well imagine the bureaucratic descriptions of Rose's plight.

Unconsciously, I began composing a speech in my head. Was there anything better than slum housing and job ghettos ahead for Rose? Even in a country like Canada with a reasonable health and social-security system, if you were born poor, the odds are that you'll still grow up hungry, lose fights, flunk school, quit trying, get pregnant, go on welfare or end up with a rotten job. What a bloody life! Was it any wonder that the underclass took to drink or drugs? Anything to deaden the pain. Even if Rose dried out, got straight and went back to school, would she have any chance at all?

Quit, I thought. Get down off the platform. Yet I couldn't help being grateful that I'd never found myself in a similar fix. Compared to Rose's, my life had been a breeze: a strict parent, dance classes, a college education, secure jobs, interrupted only by a little youthful craziness with sex, drugs and noisy bands, then a political career. My constituency provided me with problems enough to give life meaning, but nothing so far that I could not handle. Now the good little do-gooder, I needed little more than to feel useful. But to keep my busybody job, I also needed the support of people who normally did not need and did not want my help. Like that New York mayor, Ed Koch, I was always asking myself: "How am I doing?" especially with the majority who never called and couldn't even remember my name when the pollsters asked. Giving speeches to myself was no help to anybody.

I looked up at Rose's hunched shoulders. "How old are your kids?"

"Five and three."

"You said they had problems. What kind?"

"The big one sick all the time, and the little one don't talk."

"Hard drugs won't do them or the new baby any good, you know that."

"I know."

"If it's his child, you might have a claim against Norman's family."

"No. Both his parent is drunks. And they have big fight all the time."

"He told you that."

"Yeah."

I thought about that for a bit, then asked, "Is Bud still working?"

"If that what you call it."

I ignored the gibe. "Rose, did you take all Norman's clothes?"

Rose blushed. "Yeah."

"What did you do with them?"

"I put them in for cleaning."

"But he had no money to get them out!"

The housekeeper almost grinned. Almost. "Not my problem."

I shook my head. "So, he couldn't have gotten out of the room even if he'd wanted to? You people had him coming and going. He'd have been safer sleeping on the streets."

"It was just a trick. To pay him back." Rose got up and went and stood in the corner, just as she must have done as a kid in school. "I didn't do it with Norman. It not his kid."

"I see." I started to pick up my money. I counted the bills and folded them in half. Getting down on my hands and knees, I plugged in the phone. "One more thing, Rose. Have you been phoning my room? To see if I was here?"

"No."

As if on cue, the phone rang. I picked it up. "Hello . . .. Do you want to tell me who's calling? ...Who is it?"

Holding the instrument to my chest, I asked Rose, "Do you know any heavy breathers?"

The young woman made a pained face.

"Okay. Good bye." I banged down the phone.

"You can rest here for a while, if you want."

"You going to call the cops?"

"About the phone call?"

"About me?"

"No, but your next victim might. You should check yourself into a treatment centre, Rose. Get your life straight. Look after yourself and your kids." I untied my Docs and massaged my feet for a minute before slipping the shoes back on with the laces untied.

Rose touched the ring in her nose. "You hear that Lily the desk clerk died?"

"No. Where did you hear that?"

"Downstairs."

"That's too bad. Really."

"You want your bed turn down?"

I shook my head. I sorted my money and replaced it in my wallet. It was hard to believe that Rose would rob me twice in one day but I put the wallet in my skirt pocket, just in case. I took one last look at the woman sitting on my bed, then hurried out of the room.

# Chapter Twenty
## Bud, my buddy, is a baddy and a saddy

Saturday, April 1

9:10 p.m.

For most of my short legislative life, Bud Budinski had been dogging my trail. Now that I needed to talk to him, Bud might as well have playing hide and seek. In search of my man, I'd journeyed from the basement mop closet to the Rooftop Garden. Working my way down again, from haven to hall, by way of the back stairs, I checked every hallway and every open doorway.

After exhausting every other possibility, I took one last look in the lobby area. From the ceiling speaker, Madonna blessed my return with a song and a prayer. After cruising through the restaurant and the bar without any luck, I passed by the newsstand and spotted Bud ogling a nudie magazine foldout.

I knuckle-tapped the glass. Bud took a furtive look around, then clumsily folded the naked girl. Before I could corner him, he dropped the magazine back in the rack, bolted to the lobby, then darted into the men's washroom beside the elevators. Taking a deep breath I followed him in, the disinfectant stinging my nostrils as I cleared the swinging door. Inside, a fluorescent glare bounced off shiny white-tiled walls. Through watery eyes I saw that we were not alone. Manic Man stood at ease before the little boy's urinal.

At my entrance, Manic Man snapped to attention and zipped up quickly. Right away he began to loudly tell me what he thought. "I got my rights, young lady."

I cupped my hand to my ear, pretending to be hard of hearing.

Manic Man raised his voice, and I drew even closer to hear him better. "If you were my daughter...." He wagged his index finger at me and stomped out, leaving the fatherly threat hanging in the disinfected glare.

I found Bud cowering in the handicapped stall. He was squatting with his feet up on top of the toilet seat but he had not locked the door. Fortunately his sweat pants still had purchase on his waist. Taking him by the hand, I led him straight from the toilet to the elevator. He protested as we went, but only mildly. A life of dependence had taught Bud a truly Canadian deference to authority. Propping him up in the corner, I reached back and punched the CLOSE button.

Eager to please, Bud told me the latest news. "Lily passed on."

"I know, that's partly why I want to talk to you."

"Didn't do nothing. Honest." He looked like a naughty boy caught in the act.

"Now, Bud, take it easy. I just need to know a few things." I could see my pushiness nudging Bud backwards. Fearful, he regressed towards childishness. This made me feel like a scold, but I had no choice but to press him. "Tell me, Bud. When did you last see Norman?"

"Dunno." Bud turned and bowed his head, the dunce of the class.

I put my hand on his shoulder, giving it a little squeeze. "Was it before Christmas? Or after?" I felt his back stiffen.

"After."

"Long before he died?" I pulled him around so that I could see his face.

"Not long."

Lifting his chin, I asked, "How long?"

His head came up but he lowered his eyes. "Don't know."

"Where was he, when you saw him for the last time?"

He frowned as if he had missed the point of the question. "In his room."

"What were you doing in there?"

Bud's lips started to tremble.

"You weren't watching TV, were you? His TV was long gone, right?"

Bud's chin chopped the space between us.

Taking him by the shoulders, I shook him gently. "So what were you doing in his room?"

Bud twisted his head from side to side, protesting. "Helping Queenie."

"Helping Queenie do what?"

Bud started to blubber. "Giving her a hand. The handyman always helps Queenie move the furniture...."

"Move the furniture?"

"Yeah. Move it out." He lowered his eyes again.

"Whatever for?"

Because Bud didn't answer right away, I took his head in my hands, forcing him to face me again. "What for?"

His hands grabbed at my arms for support. Even as he strained to pull his head from my grasp, his fingers still clutched at my sleeves. "Told you before." Bud tightened his grip on my shirt. "It got wet."

I released him from my grip. "Wet? How did it get wet?"

"Don't know." Bud's hands dove into his back pockets.

"How did you get in?"

"The handyman has a pass key." He fumbled for a key chain in his pocket. "See."

"Show me." I poked an elevator button.

Bud looked lost. "Here?" He looked around the elevator car.

"No, I mean, show me Norman's room. I want to see it again."

"We can't go in there. It's against the law. The cops said so. Digger won't like it."

I leaned on the wall, my hand flat against the panel behind Bud's head, trapping him in the corner. "It's okay, Bud. I'll give you permission."

Bud scowled, his eyes narrowing, his mouth a straight line.

"Look, Bud, I'm a legislator, right. The legislature makes laws, and the cops make people obey them, right? So in a way the cops have to do what I say, okay? And, I say it's okay. Nobody will mind if I look around in there. Really, Bud, I'm telling you it's cool. Okay?"

"Dunno. Maybe."

"Bud, old buddy, you've certainly tested my devotion recently. Now I need your help, and you are going to help me. Okay?"

"Okay."

The elevator stopped at the fifth floor, and I steered Bud down the hall to room 505, where a yellow City Police tape obstructed the doorway. Taking Bud's key, I opened the door and ducked under the tape. Bud followed, one step behind me.

Rotten and cold, the room smelled slightly better than the last time I had seen it. I noted that the floor plan for the apartment looked much the same as my suite's though it lacked the furniture and the cleaning service that made my room bearable. Without the amenities, I thought, 505 was nothing more than a slummy box.

Outside, city life went on as usual. I looked out the grimy windows. Fifty feet below the wet streets reflected vehicular lights going back and forth. Traffics noise permeated the hotel's walls. But this was a world apart.

Someone had removed the security chain from the front door. Only a patch of unpainted wood and some ragged screw holes remained as evidence of The Apartment Hotel's security system. Slowly, I pushed open the bathroom door and looked inside. Not knowing what to expect, I was pleased to find the bathtub empty. The floor had dried out, but the linoleum tiles were permanently warped, their corners curling up like stale bread. Above the skirting along the wall ran a tide line or high-water mark. The management still had not succeeded in totally cleaning the writing from the wall, although they had made it difficult to read, especially in the evening gloom.

I tried the lock on the bathroom door. It still worked. Had Norman holed up in the water closet because it was his last patch of secure ground--his hill to die on? Water, water. What's in a name, eh? Did Norman become his name, or did his name become him? "Exactly where was Norman the last time you saw him?"

Bud pointed towards the balcony window. "Over there. In the corner."

I followed Bud's directions. "What was he doing?"

"Sitting. He was just sitting."

"Just sitting?" I glanced out through the grimy window onto the concrete balcony.

Bud came and squatted for a second on Norman's spot, then got up and moved away. "Norman didn't talk much, anymore."

"Eyes open?" I examined the soiled carpet, Norman's messy nest.

Puzzled, Bud shrugged.

"Did he have his eyes open?"

"Yeah, he watched us move the furniture."

"He watched you, eh? You took it all, the whole lot? Queenie and you?"

Bud shuffled towards the centre of the room. "His water bed and everything."

"He had a water bed?" I studied at the clean square on the carpet, where the bed must have sat.

"Yeah."

"It figures. What did you do with the bed's water?

"We let it run out on the balcony."

I threw up my hands. "What was Norman doing while you drained his water bed? Did you see him walk? Did he move around at all?"

"He was shivering." The handyman hitched up his pants. "That's all."

"Shivering?" I shook my head. "What happened when you came in?"

"He saw Queenie and went out on the balcony." Bud hung his head.

"Went? So, he was mobile. How did he get there, and what did he do out there? Come on, Bud, tell me."

"He crawled, sort of, then he just squatted like a guru."

I shook my head, again. "A guru?"

"That's what Queenie called it."

"Was he covered?"

Bud looked blank.

"Did he have a blanket?"

"He did . . . but...”

I took a step towards him. "But what?"

Bud crept back a step. "Queenie took it," he whimpered.

I kept coming. "Queenie took it. Why?"

Bud backed up to the wall. "It was wet."

"Wet? Jesus, it's freezing in here! He looked wet and cold, so you took his blanket." I glared at Bud for a moment. Then, pacing angrily, I crossed the faded wood floor in the kitchen area to the frayed carpet in the living room. "After you hauled his stuff out into the hall, did you mop the floor? Did you, Bud?"

"Yeah," he wailed.

"Why?"

"We shouldn't be in here."

"Why did you mop up, Bud? Why? Tell me, and I'll let you go."

"There was shit on the floor."

"Shit?"

"Yeah."

"On the floor?" I strode the perimeter of the room.

"Yeah."

"Was this writing on the wall back then?"

"Dunno."

"Think, Buddy, think!" I looked hard at the wall. Up close the hieroglyphics were now revealed to be a mixture of words and numbers. "Were all these scribbles here when you took his furniture?"

Bud threw a glance at the door. "Got to get out of here."

"The writing, Bud, was it here then?"

"I guess so."

"Who wrote on the wall, Bud?'

"Not me.  Honest."

"Was it Norman?"

"Yeah." Bud looked at me, pleadingly.  "I've got to go."

"So go, Bud.  Go on!" I made a move towards him, and Bud
scampered out into the hallway.  I peeled off the police tape, flung it
into the closet and kicked the door shut behind Bud.

So, here was where Norman Water spent his last days--in a grubby
little room, naked and cold.  This seemed to be eviction with extreme
prejudice.  But the kid had been housebound, practically a prisoner.
Once Rose had taken his clothes, he was probably too timid to set
foot outside his door.  Was that all of it, or was there another chapter
to the sordid story?  Queenie and Bud took his blanket, a truly a
cruel and unusual punishment.  That was a form of torture.  It had
been reason enough to get out, as fast as possible, though apparently
by that point, the kid could barely crawl.

I tried to imagine how Norman spent those last few weeks alone in
the place.  The telephone directory was the only book in the room.
Apart from scribbling on the wall, he had nothing much to do in
here, as far as I could see.  Perhaps he counted the days and nights
on a wall calendar, and checked them off one by one, or stared for
hours out the window as other people went off to work or shop.  I
pictured him counting the different kinds of cars and their colours.
He might have made little bets with himself about what next would
come around the corner.  I think that he must have known what was
at stake.  He must have known that you can only bet against yourself
for so long before you went weird with boredom.  If the next one's a
pickup truck, then I'll have a drink of water.  If a Yellow Cab comes
round the corner, then I'll lie down and go to sleep.  If a bus comes
by, then I'll live to see another day.

Surely he had been past caring about money.  He'd never shown any
sense of reality about it anyway, at least not while he'd been in the
hotel.  In the end he must have been hopelessly in debt, so hopeless
that only the dream of winning a lottery could have meant salvation.

Did he ever get angry? Of course he must have. His defence of Rose at the mayor's prayer breakfast showed a boyish sense of justice, a touch of old-fashioned gallantry even. Getting even rather than getting mad seemed his style. Me? I would have wanted to tear down the walls, kick down the door or smash the window. I puzzled why one so young would go down without a whimper, much less a bang. Even if he were faint from hunger, sick of filth, strange with loneliness, did he not want to hang on to dear life?

All I was engaged in here was disrespectful speculation. I did not know why Norman stayed, or what kept him here. I knew only that his last days must have been hellish. Look calmly at the facts, I thought. Norman Water had been a quiet, withdrawn kid, from a broken home. He liked swimming, television and video games, and didn't mind being alone. And he'd befriended a mentally handicapped man.

The key to Norman probably was his trickster's sense of justice. To every indignity, he replied in kind. About work he was totally passive and money melted in his hands but he quietly and consistently fought for some equilibrium, balance, fairness in his life. In fact, his eviction or detention may have been an attempt to kill the fight in him, but it was overkill, and Norman must have, in his own way, fought back. He had certainly tried to take the fight to the legislature by calling me here to his room.

I took another look at the scrawl wall. On the left was a mess of graffiti, mostly one-line slogans, the remnants of which were clearly legible still. "Buddy, my buddy, is a baddy and saddy." But I perceived some kind of pattern in the writing to the right. After a while, I realized that the contents of the scrawl were mostly numbers, not words, but rows and rows of numbers, running from to ceiling to floor.

When the sun came up, I would try to read Norman's numbers.

# Chapter Twenty-One
## Digger screws Queenie, Queenie screws Fern, Fern screws Lily, Lily screws Herb, Herb screws Rose, Rose screws me and I screw them all

Saturday, April 1

10:10 p.m.

I nosed around some more, opening doors and drawers, testing all the light switches. In the whole apartment, only one live bulb remained, a sixty-watter in an overhead fixture above the stove. Someone had left a book of matches on top of the stove but not much else and, apart from some furry grunge in the fruit bin, the refrigerator sat empty. Like the stove, it was unplugged.

By the phone, near the wall where Bud said Norman liked to sit, was last year's telephone directory. Huddled under the kitchen light, I let my fingers walk through the Yellow Pages. Riffling through the advertisements, something caught my eye. Here and there in the directory were markings in purple, the colour of the ink that imprinted my name and number on Norman's hand.

I looked more closely. Most of the take-out food places in the area Norman had been underlined or marked with a tick or a cross. Pizza joints, fried chicken stands, cafés offering Chinese and Canadian cuisine: someone, Norman probably, had noted all the ones in the downtown area. What was the key to the ticks and crosses in the margin? If the answer was "right" or "wrong," what was Norman's question?

Then I saw it: the universal symbol of consumer finance, a charge card logo. The marks graded neither the food nor the service, but their accessibility. If the advertisement indicated that the business accepted "major credit cards," then Norman had marked it with a tick.

He had ticked some outlets several times. Was this evidence of special approval? Perhaps these establishments didn't bother to phone the card company to okay purchases. Dozens of restaurants had multiple markings, demonstrating multiple use or, maybe, a measure of special appreciation. Some had several ticks followed by a single cross beside the telephone number. I figured these must indicate Norman's vanishing credit at places where he had previously charged items to his card.

Besides the names of a couple of restaurants, Norman had written the names of certain dishes: Hawaiian pizza and egg foo yung. These must have been his favourites. The handwriting seemed juvenile, the characters, like the author, unformed, unsettled and sloping backwards. I remembered that my name and number had been written on his right hand. It should have been obvious to me. Norman was a southpaw.

The boy obviously didn't know how to cook or care to know. Had he been too lazy or had they never taught him at home? I wondered why he hadn't picked up some pointers while working in the hotel kitchen, but when I pictured Norman up to his elbows in soapy water, I figured he'd had his back to the cooks most of the time. The secrets of their trade were safe from this boy.

I flipped some more pages and found more purple marks in the section called Escort Services. The boy had put question marks beside several agencies and crosses by others. Or were they kisses? One operation had a check mark beside its number and inscribed below, in thick purple print, the word, Orchid, underlined, twice.

Here was a side of Norman I hadn't seen before. He must have been unspeakably lonely and likely love matches at The Apartment Hotel were few but, for sure, TV had taught him that everything was for sale.

I stared at the Yellow Pages for a minute, totally lost in thought. Don't be crazy, Regina, I told myself. A moment later, that thought was replaced by: You can't stop now.

Outside, the headlights were still peering into the black night, cars coming and going up and down the street, engines racing at the intersection, driving couples to dinners and dates. Nobody down there cared what was happening up here.

Picking up the phone, I heard a sizzling sound on the line then, after a second, a dial tone. I dialled the number. A woman answered. I cupped my hand over the mouthpiece. "Can you tell me about your service?" I asked.

"Are you in a hotel?"

"The Apartment Hotel."

"We know it well. The price is one hundred dollars for half an hour. The tip is extra. Are you looking for a boy or a girl?"

Biting my tongue, I said, "Orchid."

The woman covered the phone, consulted with someone, then came back on the line. "You're in luck. Orchid is available tonight. Will that be cash or credit card?"

My lips dried. "Cash, I guess."

"And your name and room number?"

I had to think for a second about that little white lie. "Norman, room 505."

"Thank you Ms. Norman, your date will be there in a few minutes."

I hung up the phone and wiped my hands on my skirt. Now the escort agency thinks I'm a lesbian named Mrs. Norman waiting for a blind date with a woman named Orchid. God, what a trip. For several long minutes I debated whether to call back and cancel the appointment. Something like this was way too risky. News of this date would confirm my opponent's meanest slanders, and, God, what would my father think? Anyway what could I gain by this escapade? Maybe I should let Dr. Corbeau handle it. Corbeau and Spud. But would they ask the right questions--So, Orchid, when did you first meet Norman? What did he want? What did you do for him?

I had almost made up my mind to cancel when, pacing past the bathroom, I remembered Norman dead in the bath. Almost everywhere in the hotel I'd heard, or overheard, music, except in this room. Here, it was quiet, too quiet. My brain racing, I tried to think through the questions I needed answered. What would this Orchid know anyway? And what would she tell me? I paced up and down, until I heard the knock on the door.

Flipping off the light switch, I pulled open the door and the escort stepped inside. Leaving the door ajar to let in light from the hall, I turned to meet the blonde in a veil and a long white dress, a bit like a wedding gown.

I was remembering k.d. lang appearing on TV in a get-up like this when the woman stepped across the threshold, lifted the veil and give me a big surprise. "Fern!"

"You?" Fern danced sideways. "I never figured y'all for a dike."

My fingers combed through my hair. "I'm not."

"What's this then, sugar?" Fern brushed the back of her hand across my cheek.

The hand felt surprisingly warm but I tried to look supremely cool by planting my hands on my hips. "Look, I've been trying to find out what happened to Norman Water. I found your work name and number highlighted in his phone book." I nodded at the phone book. "So I called."

"I see." Fern looked around the dark room. "What happened to the boy's stuff?"

"The staff took it away for cleaning." I surprised myself at the ease with which I parroted The Apartment Hotel's official line.

Fern fanned her nose. "Girl, it needed it."

"So, you did know Norman, after all?"

"Not really, not real well. We had a few dates, that's all."

"Dates? Is that really what they're called?"

"Sure, Baby. Like so." Fern reached up and touched my face again.

I turned my cheek. "Did you sleep with him?"

"Sleep?" The blonde laughed, a rich, mocking laugh. "No way."

"I mean: did you have sex with him?"

"Y'all mean, did I fuck him? Is that it, girl?"

Blanching slightly, I nodded. "Yes."

"Then, say it, honey."

I looked her straight in the face. "Did you fuck him?"

Fern laughed at me. "No."

"No?"

"Not exactly, girl. The boy paid me to hold him and talk to him."

Humbled, I hid my hands in my pockets. "You mean hugs?"

"Sure. Lots of men are like that, half my regulars, but that boy Norman was a really sad case. That poor chump used to complain that he might as well be invisible because folks looked right through him, like he wasn't there."

I stole a glance at the bathroom door. "Did he ever talk about anything else?"

"No. That boy just put his head on my mamms. I put my lovin' arms around him and rocked him like a baby. Y'all know what I mean."

"That's sad." I dragged my hands through my hair again, then, catching myself, I folded my arms across my chest. "Why did you stop seeing him?"

"He got cut off when his credit ran out. It's business, not love, girl.

You know what they say: 'Business is business, and love is bullshit.'"

"If you don't mind my asking, when did he last call you?"

"Oh, quite a while back."

"Be more precise. When was that?"

"It must have been November. I was not sorry, I can tell you. Y'all know, I don't really dig doing dates in my place of work."

"Why? Was it against Greenwood's rules?"

Fern gave me a long look. "It was an issue, sure. That boy Norman kept calling me down in the bar. So I came by a couple of times without telling the agency."

"Room service."

"Right, but bad news, that was. Then that little twat Rose barged in one day and caught us together."

"What happened? Did she rat you out to the management?"

Fern ditched the latter idea with a dismissive wave. "Rose moved right in and tapped the boy out. She tried to get him to go and get a job; he tried to kick her out of his bed. Typical marriage, you know."

With a glance at Fern's gown, I asked, "Did he ever play any tricks on you?"

"Tricks?" Fern considered the question, then glanced at her white gown. "Yeah, he did. He ruined a brand-new cocktail dress, if that's what you mean."

"With the lipstick kiss on your ass?"

"Y'all heard about that did you? You just can't keep a secret around here. Well, it just shows how careful a career girl has to be."

I walked over to the balcony window and looked at my own pale reflection in the glass. "How did you two meet?" I asked.

"How did we meet? Girl, it wasn't very romantic, you know. Not at all. He sent out for a girl, and, lucky me, I got the call. I didn't want to do it because of my other job here, but the boss bitch said she had no one else on duty. At the time, I didn't know Norman was a 'perm,' you know, a permanent resident. He'd never come into the bar while I was on shift, so I had no idea really. I guess he didn't drink liquor. Anyhow, no big problem until he got fired. I paid him a bit to use his room for a week or two, but then he got honkie about me using it and locked me out. The hotel management eventually got wind of the whole business and turned up the heat to get him out."

I looked up, sharply. "Turned up the heat?"

"Sure."

"They didn't actually turn on the heat, did they?"

"It's just an expression."

"More likely, they turned the heat off."

"Whatever." Fern shrugged and looked at her watch. So, that's it. We've had our little talk?"

"I'm amazed that people pay you simply to talk."

"Why the big surprise, girl? Isn't that what they pay you to do?"

I laughed but felt momentarily speechless. "It's not quite the same."

"A real political pro." Coming at me from behind, Fern put her hands on my waist. I stiffened but did not try to free myself until Fern began nuzzling the nape of my neck.

I pushed the blonde away. "Look, I'm sorry. You are beautiful but I'm not gay."

"You sure about that, honey?" Fern purred. I backed away to the wall. Reaching behind my neck, the blonde pulled me face forward and covered my mouth with a kiss. I struggled, then broke free, gasping for breath.

Stepping towards the doorway, Fern looked at her watch. "Okay, your time's up, girl. One hundred dollars plus tip." She stuck out her palm.

Reaching for my wallet, I counted out five twenties and handed them over.

Fern put out her hand again. "Tip!"

I ignored it. "That's all you're getting, Fern. I don't usually have to pay people to talk to me!"

"Don't forget the caresses, and the kiss. You liked that, I could tell. That should be at least $100 more."

"Forget it. I can get my own kisses."

"That's your final position?"

"It is."

"You sure?"

"Get out of here!" I held the door open for her.

"Suit yourself." Fern turned on her toes and sashayed out the door.

Heading for the balcony, I yanked open the sliding glass door and went outside. I wiped my mouth with my hand. My fingers were trembling like twigs in a thunderstorm and my supper-time soup was not sitting well in my stomach. Did I go too far this time, I wondered.

# Chapter Twenty-Two
## Rose + Fern + Lily / Digger = Queenie

Saturday, April 1

11:02 p.m.


I clutched the balcony rail, gulping down night air. I undid the top button on my shirt and unlaced my Docs. I breathed deeply, trying to calm myself. Cursing my recklessness, I locked the sliding-glass door went back inside. Someone knocked on the door and, thinking it might be Fern again, I yanked it open. But there in the doorway stood not Fern but Queenie. And, behind her, Bud Budinski.

Queenie pressed the flat of her hand on my breastbone and shoved me roughly back into the room. "When I spotted Fern coming out of Norman's old room, I wondered who she might be seeing in there. Then good old Bud told me it was you. Was I surprised? Pleasantly surprised, mind you, but surprised all the same. Now, this little escapade is going to cost you dearly, my dear."

Trying to keep my feet, I stumbled and fell on my rear. "Cost me? What for?" I scrambled to get up but, instead, fell down again. One of my Docs came off.

Queenie kicked the shoe aside and loomed over my supine form. "Apparently, you called a call girl to your room--well, not your room exactly--but a hotel room anyway, one you were not supposed to be in."

"So what. We just talked." I struggled to get to my feet. "And I paid her well for that."

"Fornicate, deviate, communicate: It doesn't really matter." Queenie lifted her heavy hand so that it hung over my head. "So, I'd say you are going to give me some money, honey. Give me the money.

Please."

At Queenie's side, Bud snickered and repeated the message, echoing his master's voice. "Give me money, honey."

Pushing myself up onto my elbows and heels, I crab-walked out of their way. Flopping over onto my hands and knees, I stood up shakily and retreated by tiny limping steps towards Norman's corner of the room. In frustration, I kicked off the other shoe.

Puffing herself up, Queenie smiled and showed me a fist. "What do you say to $1,000?"

Now quite excited, Bud shouted even louder, "1,000!"

"No." I put my back to the wall. "No way!"

Queenie slammed her fist into her spare hand. "Pay!" she snapped.

"For what?" I shot back. "What for?"

Queenie straight-armed my breastbone again. "You've had your fun, now you must pay your money"

"Fun?" I tried to laugh in her face. "Interviewing a witness? What fun was that?"

"You had your fun, pay your money," Bud screamed and waved his fist, just like his mentor.

"You had Fern, sorry, Orchid--in one of our hotel rooms," Queenie touch her eyelid with her index finger. "I saw her. I'm the witness."

"I'm a witness too." Buddy added.

"Screw you and your other witness." Glaring at Bud, I folded my arms across my chest, ready to stand my ground.

Pumping herself up for a big speech, Queenie took a deep breath, then another. "Listen, you political piglet, the only thing you have worth anything is your good name, but, if you don't pay, that name will be mud when the media hear about your little trick."

A tide of blood went out of my face. "What?"

"Queer politician hires whore. Now, I imagine that would a big story. And all because you refused to pay a little hush money."

"I'm not paying you a damn thing!." My voice was breaking with rage. I swallowed hard. "Nothing, not a penny, you sick creep."

"Pay me or you're finished." Queenie swaggered back and forth in front of me, while, behind her back, Bud aped her every move.

I shook my head. "Now I've heard everything: a penny-ante bouncer is worried about my reputation."

"Bouncer?" Queenie froze, as if nobody before had ever dared insult her directly.

"You have a smart accent and smart clothes but, deep down, you are really just a dumb thug, aren't you?"

Easing off her dinner jacket, Queenie handed it to Bud. Then she lifted her hands, dropped her head and went into a boxer's crouch. "Sorry about this, madam, but sometimes you really piss people off." Queenie shuffled towards me. She feinted with her left, and I flinched.

Queenie laughed at my fear. "If you're so smart, why are you so scared?"

I couldn't stop myself. "A thug and an idiot."

Queenie glanced over her shoulder. "She's talking about you, Bud."

"You're the idiot.".

Queenie planted her shiny pumps squarely in front of me, clenched her fists and stood there with her jaw muscles tensing.

"You want to hit me, don't you?"

"Oh, yes."

"You want to plough your fist into my guts."

"You read my mind."

"You want to smash my head against the wall, put the boots to me, then leave me whimpering on the floor, don't you?"

Queenie breathed heavily through her teeth. "Do I ever."

I looked hard into her deadly black eyes. "Does talking about it help at all?"

"I'd much rather punch your face in."

"Even you are not that thick."

Queenie was primed like a grenade but, by inhaling deeply and airing out her lungs, she kept her rage from exploding. In those tense seconds, I was conscious of Bud wheezing a few feet behind his heavy breathing mentor. Suddenly Queenie jabbed the air in front of my face and I shrank back against the wall. She punched the air again and I stumbled getting out of her way. Falling, I bumped my head on the skirting board and was dazed for a second or two.

Queenie gave a heavy sigh. "Sometimes, I hate this bloody job, but I do so love the violence. I should have been a cop."

Bud laughed and Queenie smiled in his direction.

"You don't get it do you, Queenie. What you've done is criminal. It's called attempted extortion and it will get you jailed or deported or both."

"Nothing happened."

"Nothing."

"Not yet."

"Yet?"

"You can leave now," Queenie said to me.

"You first," I said as I struggled to my feet.

"No, I insist."

"No, I want to look around some more." How I got the words out I don't know because I was feeling really rough.

"The cops won't like it."

"So call the cops. I'll be waiting for them right here."

Queenie drew a long slow breath, then stepped forward, forcing me back to the wall. She towered over me, looking hard at me with her nostrils flaring. "Listen, I probably should not have threatened you. Sorry about that, but you did ask for it. Now, we both need some time to cool down. So, here's my proposal. I'm going to leave here for a while. Take some time to think about your future--with or without your political career. In the morning, I'm going to come by your room. If you have my money, then we'll forget all about this little incident. I won't tell your reporter friend about your little assignation and you will say nothing to Digger about what went on here. All right?"

She let me go and my body slid down the wall. As I was going down, Queenie suddenly kicked my feet out from under me and I banged my head on the floor again.

Bud had become very excited. "Can I have this room now? Can I, Queenie?"

My gut was screaming with pain and my head hurt too.

"You said I could have Norman's room if I helped you."

"Later, Bud. Later. We need to leave the lady in peace. Let's go." Queenie put on her dinner jacket.

I lay on the floor gasping for breath.

"Queenie, you said I could have it."

Suddenly, without warning, I vomited up my dinner. I watched helplessly as the puke splattered over my shirt and skirt.

Queenie looked at me with disgust. "Next time, use the toilet."

Bud giggled. "Use the toilet."

"Buddy, unplug the phone and bring it with you. That's a good chap. You see; you're not as slow as they say." Queenie turned out the light. I heard the door open then close.

Putting my hands flat on the carpet, I pushed myself back to wall. I tried sitting up straight, but was too groggy and sore. It must have been that godawful cold potato soup, I thought. Or fear. Colwell's formula: Food poisoning and naked fear equals puke. I struggled to get up on my hands and knees, then I passed out.

When I came round it was very dark and very quiet. And I was shivering, whether from toxic soup, shock or cold was not at all clear to me. I dragged myself to my feet and tried walking around to get warm but my legs were too wobbly and I had to sit down again. I sat and stared at the graffiti wall, trying to see through the black to make something out of it.

After a few minutes, my curiosity got the better of me and I remembered the book of matches on the stove. Crawling into the kitchen, I pulled down the oven door and pushed myself within reach of the stove top. I fished around for the matches and found them but then accidentally knocked them onto the floor. I fumbled around on the floor until I found them. Matches in hand, I made my way back across the carpet to the scrawl wall.

Sitting on my butt, I struck a match and tried to read the wall. I could make out a few of the numbers but the matches gave off too little light for me to see the big picture. I tried moving around and lit four matches before I gave up. The match box had only a couple left and I figured I might need them later, to start a fire or something.

Patience, I told myself. Wait until the sun comes up. I lay on my back with my arms wrapped around my trunk and tried to think. I thought about the provincial legislature and yesterday's question period but yesterday seemed like such a long time ago. My question had been about the homeless and how apartments like this one were being replaced by hotels. The Apartment Hotel's instant makeover had not been exactly what I had in mind at the time. Still, it was obviously part of the problem, not the solution, despite what "Dandy" Lyon had to say about private sector solutions, the Apartment Hotel wasn't helping the poor or the homeless--quite the opposite.

What about Lyon anyway? The minister had been strangely defensive about my suggestion that he was looking after his own interests, rather than the public's. His Question of Privilege had certainly gotten us off the subject of the homeless, shelters and public housing. That could have been an accident but, in politics, it was safer to assume that nothing ever happened by accident. Lyon was a professional politician, the political minister for this city, no less--the Tory in charge of everything from local patronage to election strategies. He played to win. And as a rule, he did not make careless mistakes. Idly, I wondered what he would think of the Apartment Hotel and if he had an inkling of what was going on here.

Moss had discovered that Greenwood had once been the subject of a commercial fraud investigation and he had lost his position with a firm of chartered accountants. From what I'd seen of the man's work Greenwood was certainly capable of dubious money-making schemes. If Norman Water was as good with numbers as his teacher claimed, he might have uncovered something fishy in the hotel's accounts. If so, why was Greenwood trying so hard to throw him out onto the cold streets? Crazy as it might seem, if he had something on Greenwood, the smart thing would be to keep Norman around, either as an employee or as a tenant. But Norman's pranks had made continued employment or permanent residence nearly impossible.

A chill had crept right through my body. Fumbling in the dark, I made my way back to the kitchen stove. I tried setting the dial to BAKE and cranked the temperature dial up all the way, but the appliance was stone dead. Queenie must have cut the power. I looked around but there seemed to be no way to get warm. I could try crawling upstairs to my room but, if I did that, I might not be able to get back inside Norman's squat and I wanted to be here when the sun came up. Those scribbles on the wall might have a story to tell.

When I curled myself up into a ball, my stomach did not hurt as much. And after a while I must have fallen dead asleep.

# Chapter Twenty Three
## I've lost track of the days--
## will that count against me?

Sunday, April 2

After midnight

An hour or two later I awoke to find myself shivering in a gummy pool of drool, vomit and blood. The blood seemed to have leaked from the base of my skull while I was sleeping. I hoped that my scalp would not need stitches. My head throbbed and my stomach ached something terrible. I sat up and massaged my neck, turning my head this way and that, trying to get the stiffness out of the muscles.

In a room down the hall a toddler cried. "Om-mee, Om-mee."

Slowly it dawned on me that, so far, I had succeeded in only one thing. I had managed to put myself completely into Norman Water's corner. Here I lay in his apartment, like him, bruised, frozen and sick to the stomach, waiting for the next horrible thing to happen.

The room had grown so cold I could now see my breath fog in the dark. Rolling over, I crawled about on my hands and knees searching for my missing shoes. With some effort I found one but that gave me only one Doc to hop about with. When I tried standing, my legs felt rubbery, but by propping myself against the wall I slowly maneuvered myself about.

Staggering over to the thermostat, I flicked the control lever back and forth, but nothing happened. I pulled off the plastic cover and tried again. With the tip of my finger, I jiggled the mercury switch inside, but the spark of life was gone. I let the cover slip from my fingers onto the carpet.

My head ached and my mouth felt bone dry. I was so thirsty. And tired.

Hand over hand, I passed myself along the wall, moving blindly towards the bathroom. Reaching in, I flicked the light switch, but, of course, nothing happened. When I leaned clumsily on the door, it banged against the bathtub. Stumbling up to the sink, I peered into the bathroom mirror, trying to recognize myself in the gloomy reflection. Not a pretty sight, I thought. Tentatively, I felt for bumps on my head and found one but it was more of a gash. In falling after Queenie's threat, I had split my head open and my hair was sticky with blood.

A tap dripped. A tear for Norman Water? Another drip, one for Regina Colwell. I turned on the tap, cupped my hands to take a drink and spat it out, quickly. The water tasted stale and rusty, as if it had been in the pipes a long time. I turned the tap on full until I had sluiced all the brown gunk away. Scooping up some fresh water in my hands, I gently lowered my face into the liquid. Twisting my head so that the water could wash over my wound and through my hair, I let the water do its work. As it touched the damaged flesh, I winced, the cold chilling my wounds and sharpening the pain.

I washed most of the blood and puke off my face and hair then stood, leaning over the sink, shivering. The hot water tap was difficult to turn but, when it came on, I had heat. I stood for a minute, bathing my hands in the warm water. I was frozen. My body needed warmth.

Turning my head, I stared down at the bath, Norman's bath and, beside it, the half-empty bottle of Lysol on the floor. Norman would not mind. I lowered myself to my knees and turned on the hot water tap, then the cold. With shaky hands I sloshed Lysol and water around the tub, washing away the last remnants of Norman Water's dead skin, dried sweat and thirsty tears. I put in the plug, filled the tub, then pulled the plug again, rinsing any faint residue of the previous occupant down the drain. Reinserting the rubber stopper, I ran myself a hot bath.

While the tub was filling, it occurred to me to take off my shirt and

One Woolly in order to rinse away the puke. Laying the cotton shirt flat on the bottom of the sink, I turned the taps on full power. I scrubbed and rubbed until the shirt was almost clean then hung it on the bathroom door to dry. With Woolly One I was more selective and tried to steer the wool under the tap, so that the water soaked only the soiled parts.

With my arms resting on the rim off the bathtub and my chin on my hands, I watched the water rise until the bath was half full. I gingerly lowered my shivering body into the water. Blood rushed to all the sore places on my body, my ribs, my guts and my head, and I groaned. But, after a while, the heat worked its soothing way, warming my bones, smoothing the hard edge off all the aches.

Here I am, I numbly thought, immersing my body in Norman Water's bath, baptizing myself in his wake. As I soaked in the warm water, the notion slowly sank in that I could quite literally lie here for the rest of my life. I closed my eyes and rested, letting the bath cool slowly, by degrees. Entropy's darling.

Lounging in the tub, I passed out again for a moment and dreamed briefly, until a vivid nightmare disturbed my rest. In my sleep I imagined that Norman Water had transformed himself into the French revolutionary, Jean Paul Marat, and that I had become the damaged aristocrat, Charlotte Corday. Marat lay in his bath, scribbling calls to arms, while Corday crept up on him with a knife. Just as I was about to strike the fatal blow, I awoke with a start. The dream was all wrong. The parts were mixed up, the roles reversed. I could not be Corday. I had to be Marat. No, that was not right. Norman had become Marat, and I had turned into a Norman imitator.

My right arm had gone to sleep lying immobile for too long on the rim of bathtub. I lifted the tingling limb off the tub and massaged it until I'd restored the circulation. I tried to lever myself out of the water, but fell back in with a splash. I was so stiff that my body could hardly move. I ran some more hot water.

I lay on my back, thinking about how to pass the time until daylight. After a few minutes the silence started to unnerve me, so I began to hum to myself. In the late-night movies, the heroes--trapped miners or condemned prisoners--sang to each other to get themselves through the long hours before daylight. I had only myself to sing to, and it was not enough.

I thought of some songs I'd heard on alternative radio--the anarchist band, Propaghandi's "HEAD, chest or FOOT," Bif Naked's "Never Alone" or Radiohead's "the bends" but I could not remember many of the lyrics. Even Bif's came hard:

"A little determination and a little more pride

A little determination will ease your pain inside

LET ME TELL YOU

THAT YOU'RE NEVER ALONE

YEAH, YEAH"


So did Propaghandi's:

"I'd rather be imprisoned

 in a George Orwell-ian World,

than this pacified society

 of happy boyz and gurlz."


Mostly, I could only come up with an opening line or two. Was this politician getting out of touch, I wondered? Face it, I thought, your job doesn't allow much time for listening to music any more. Politics was making me old and I was not yet thirty. Next thing I knew, I'd be listening to golden oldies.

My thoughts returned to the problem of filling the hours until dawn. I just needed to wait. Norman, after all, had waited here alone, for weeks on end.

Then my feelings of frustration and anger got the better of me. I started to think about what happened to Norman, and to me, both left damaged and alone in an empty, dirty apartment, and I came to boil again. Nobody could call it a civilized society, if it let a kid be starved out of his home or a woman be beaten up for money. Surely even this city's fathers and mothers wouldn't let them get away with that shit, would they?

I tried to sit up and winced from the pain in my guts.

I had almost exactly replicated Norman's situation. Alone in his room, his bath, his water, just like him. Alone and friendless, with no light or heat or telephone. Was this how it ended for you, Norman: alone, freezing in the dark and up to your neck in dirty water? Dead anyway, with my name on his hand.

A mad thought popped into my head. My situation was uncannily like Norman's, almost as if it had been stage-managed. What if Norman was playing his final prank from beyond the grave? Maybe he'd calculated all the possibilities. Maybe he planned that I'd find my way here, that I'd phone for Orchid, that I'd bust my guts to do my job. Was this his final payback, his revenge on the Apartment Hotel? I now knew that Bud had given Norman my name. So, it was not such a crazy idea after all.

Good old Bud, who watched and cheered while a bouncer extortionist threatened me. I, who went to no ends to help my constituents, had failed absolutely in Bud's case. My recent dealings with Bud might give me real cause to reflect hard on my mission in life. The events of the last few days were forcing me to see service to my constituents in a new light.

Yes, my work gave me a purpose in life. Without it I might be as miserable as the employees in this crappy hotel. Yet I was also coming to realize that I thrived on Bud's kind of dependency. I needed him to need me as much as he had once needed me. I wanted my constituents' loyalty; I wanted their votes. I was thinking that I'd become a vote slut.

In this respect was I any different from a coke dealer, a downtown pimp or a TV preacher? As Digger Greenwood might say, the only difference was in our bottom lines, dollars versus votes. Maybe Digger had dug the more honest path, after all. He didn't care a damn if people liked him or not. He cared only if they paid their way or worked for their pay. "Nothing personal" might be his motto, if he hadn't already selected "Me first."

But, thinking it over, I still couldn't explain why, in the first place, Digger had objected to giving me a room. That bit of business was still something of a mystery. His motive had to be personal pique or a political point, one or the other. It had to be something more than Greenwood's party games, Australian rules.

I must try to think. When Corbeau showed me this bath, it had been way less than half empty. Trying to remember the precise details of that scene, I stared at the ceiling. Only a pale light shone through the window from the street outside. The light barely reached beyond the living room into the bathroom but something on the ceiling caught my eye. Something up there demanded a closer look.

With great tenderness towards my aching stomach, I lifted myself out of the water. Carefully, I stretched my arms up over my head. A stab of pain shot through my innards and I gripped my side with one hand. Then I climbed carefully onto the toilet seat to take a closer look at the sprinkler nozzle on the ceiling.

I found it hard to make out anything in the dark, but the closer I looked, I felt sure something about the sprinkler looked peculiar. Those were scorch marks around the nozzle. I sat on the toilet seat, my head in my hands, thinking about room 505. No heat, no light, no phone. And no water? When the sun comes up, I must have another, closer look at this. I got back into the bath.

For a long time, I kept refilling the bath with hot water. But, as my dad likes to say, one can get too much of a good thing. Eventually, I let the bath water get cold. My skin was starting to shrivel like a prune anyway.

My clothes were not really dry yet but I chose to employ the body heat method to finish the job. Dressed in my damp shirt and my wet-smelling wool skirt, I went and sat on the living room carpet. With my arms around my knees I waited. My heart soared at the false dawn but I had to wait an unbearably long time before the sun came round from the back of the Apartment Hotel and crept into Norman's window.

In a nearly dream-like state, I watched the first ray of sunlight seep into the room then slowly expand into a brightness that filled the room from floor to ceiling. When the light fell on the graffiti and hieroglyphics, I got up for a closer look.

Yes, there were words, and numbers.

Before the hotel staff washed them off, Norman had half filled the wall with these numbers. He had written long columns of numbers, which stretched from the skirting up to the six foot level and along the length of the wall. On this occasion, I thought it excellent that the staff had not done that good a job because the numbers were still visible. True, they were hard to read, even in bright sunlight. But it could be done, I was sure.

Now, I could see that each column had two rows. The row on the left consisted of simple numbers from one to sixty or so. But, in one or two rows, this sequence was broken by the addition of extra numbers. In one column it was 31a and 31b. At first glance, the configuration seemed quite peculiar, but, at the same time, strangely familiar.

Then I came to the fifth column and, gradually, the lights went on in my head. I knew these numbers. They were not just any old numbers. I got it. These were my numbers! They were the poll results from the last election. Next to my numbers were Hightucker's from the constituency to the east of mine. My brain was spinning.

I counted the columns and realized there were twenty in all. But the city had only ten constituencies. Then I realized that the left-hand numbers were polling station numbers. The numbers 31a and 31b represented an area that had grown since the previous election and which had been divided into two polls. Still, that did not explain the twenty sets. So, why twenty?

The first ten columns represented the results in the city's constituencies at the last provincial election. But what were the next ten? They could not be rural constituencies, because they had too many polls and too many voters in each poll. Nor could they belong to the other big city in the province because it had less than ten constituencies. I figured there must be some connection between the first ten and the second but I just could not see it.

Then it came to me. Bingo! I knew exactly what been going on. Norman had figured out Greenwood's game. Maybe just maybe, Norman had brought me here to uncover it. Well done, Norman Water!

I looked out the window. Cars were starting to move in the street below.

But what had happened to Norman? I paced the floor from bathroom to balcony door and back. Why did he die in his bath? I picked the last of the matches off the living room carpet and rushed back into the bathroom. Peeling back a match, I tore it from the book. I scraped the match across the striking surface three times, shredding the match in the process, but failing to light it. Clambering back onto the toilet seat, I pulled the last match from the book. I held the tip between my thumb and the book, and yanked. The match flared, and I held it up to the nozzle. The flame quickly burned down to my fingers, the fire nipping at my nails. I held on for as long as I could, dropping the match only when the fire alarm out in the hall started ringing.

The clapper on the alarm struck three times, then a few drops of water dribbled out of the overhead nozzle. I looked up, and the dribble became a shower. The water poured down on my head, onto the walls and into the bathtub. I watched the spray splatter my bath water, then lifted my head into the spray and tried to wash away fatigue. The shower displaced a thought from depths of my brain and an old science lesson swam to the surface of my mind. "Eureka!" I croaked. "Eureka!" Then I laughed until my stomach started to hurt even more.

I had the answer. At last, I knew how Norman's furniture got wet. Now I knew how Norman had died, cold and lonely in this pit of a room. I knew how, and why. Norman had figured it out, but the kid had been too smart for his own good. Now, I promised myself, I had to ensure that this girl was not going to get trapped by the same merciless animals.

Slipping into my Doc Martens, I went to the door and put my ear to the wood. Outside people trotted down the halls to the fire exits. I put my eye to the peephole and watched them pass. Waiting until they had all gone by, I opened the door a crack and peeked out. Look to the left, look right, then left again, I recited in my head. The hall looked empty. Go for it, I told myself. I dashed down the corridor, through the fire door and up the concrete stairs, two storeys, to my room.

Breathless, I arrived at 701 and fumbled in my skirt pocket for the key. Cursing myself, I realized that I must have dropped it somewhere. I hammered on the door with both hands. "Rose! ROSE! It's me. Let me in."

No answer. The cleaning cart Rose had left by my door was gone. And Rose with it probably. Damn. But if I couldn't get into my room, I had better go down and have another chat with Digger Greenwood.

Pushing open the fire door at the end of the corridor, I stepped out onto the back stairs. Thinking myself the last person to leave the hotel, I was not surprised to find myself alone in the concrete stairwell. Because I did not believe that the fire department would respond very quickly, I jogged rather than ran.

And, just to make sure that the wrong people didn't destroy the evidence, I needed to cover my tracks. So, on the way down, I stopped on every floor to pull the fire alarm and turn on the fire hoses. On the seventh floor, I watched as the fire hose filled with water, then snaked uncontrollably as it sprayed the ceiling, walls and floors. For the rest, I do not stop long. I pulled the fire alarms, cranked on the water in the hoses and rushed down to the next floor.

# Chapter Twenty Four
## Talking to yourself--even more boring than listening to the CBC

Sunday, April 2

Sunday, 6:20 a.m.


By the time I reached the ground floor and the door to the lobby, little rivulets of water were running at my feet. The water from the hoses was gathering on the steps, leaking through the carpets in the hallways and following the law of gravity down the stairs. Pity.

Crossing the lobby, I spotted the crowd of evacuees on the driveway outside and stepped lightly to avoid being seen by them. Reaching Greenwood's office, I tried the door. The handle turned, so I peaked inside. No Greenwood. Good.

I stepped in so that I could look behind the door but the marked constituency map was gone. Nothing ventured, nothing gained. I searched the office but saw no sign of it in the pile of files or inside the desk drawer. I knew I had not made a mistake. I'd seen the map when I was checking in but Greenwood had it well hidden now. My bet was that Norman had seen it as well. In all likelihood, he had found the numbers on Greenwood's desk but, only later, when he'd transcribed them onto his apartment wall, did he figure out what they meant.

Somewhat disappointed I stepped back out into the hallway, preparing to recross the lobby, when my nose picked up a nasty smell. I sniffed and looked around. Smoke was drifting out of the restaurant. Darting inside, I marched towards the kitchen. Inside, the french fryer was a raging grease fire. The hot fat was bubbling wildly, with flames roaring on the surface and black smoke billowing up to the ceiling.

Some cook had responded to the fire alarm without turning off the fryer, and it was now way too hot for me to touch the controls. For a second, the fire alarm paused and the sprinklers dried up, then the grease fire set them both off again. Somewhere in the back of my mind, I remembered that water was the worst thing for grease fires. I momentarily wondered if I should search for a chemical extinguisher and smother the fatty fire but quickly rejected that idea. Call me irresponsible but I had no time and, besides, the fire-fighters were surely on their way.

I had to get to Greenwood's room on the staff floor. To reach that destination I now had to face the slow trudge nineteen floors up the concrete stairs. Going down had definitely been easier, I thought. To hell with the fire regulations, I thought, as I stepped into the elevator and sent the machine for a ride to the nineteenth floor. Just as the doors opened at the top, the alarm stopped. I needed more time so pulled the nineteenth floor alarm and started the fire hose spraying in the hallway.

I had not been to Greenwood's room before but no one could mistake it. On the door was only one number, a prime number, 1. And, to make my life easier, the door was open. I pushed my way through and was surprised by the room's decor. Downstairs, Greenwood's office was cramped and busy. Upstairs in his private domain, it was sparse and empty. The walls, carpets and curtains were all snow white. Except for another upside-down Quantas poster in the kitchen area, I saw no prints on the wall or decorative ornaments around the furniture. Indeed, the furnishings were minimal. A couple of stools stood beside the kitchen nook and a low wide bed against the back wall. No tables, no chairs, no visitors. On the floor besides the bed was a scattering of Madonna CDs.

The room seemed too neat, too tidy, and too quiet. My nose picked up a whiff of Greenwood's after-shave lotion but he appeared not to be home. Out of the corner of my eye I thought I saw something move near the window. Then a voice startled me.

"Out here," Greenwood yelled. He was outside on the balcony, standing at the rail in his bathrobe, staring, without benefit of his eyeglasses, at an incredible early morning view of the city. He lazily beckoned me to join him. So, I did. We could ignore fire regulations together.

Without a word, Greenwood reached over with one hand and tilted my head so that he could examine it for damage. With his free hand, he parted my wet hair, pulling strands free from the scab on my scalp.

"Queenie?"

"Queenie."

"Don't know if it'll make any difference but I fired her ass when I heard about it from Bud."

"She's gone?"

"Gone."

I fell silent and closed my eyes for a minute.

Greenwood touched my eyelids. "Tired?"

"I'm thinking."

"What about?"

"Norman Water."

"Norman, the annoying kid in 505? Quit worrying about him. Visit us after we've redecorated the room, and you'll never know he was there. Forget him, Regina. Water was an absolute zero." Greenwood gave me a matey slap on the shoulder. "Live for the day."

"Live for the day, eh, Mr. Greenwood? No past, no memory, no guilt?"

"You got it."

I folded my arms across my chest and looked down at the driveway nineteen floors below. "Nobody should die like Norman did. Nobody should have to live like he did either."

"You always like this in the morning?" he snapped.

"Always," I snapped back.

"Remind me not to marry you."

"No need." I swiped a loose hair away from my eyes and treated Greenwood to a minute of silence, while my fingertips carefully probed the abrasion at the back of my head. "Who owns this place?"

"What?"

"Who are the owners?"

"A couple of developers, the Ford dealer down the way, some dentists and a lawyer. Although you might say they're only renting it from the bank. It's mortgaged right up to the Rooftop Garden. Why?"

"So what's in it for you?"

He waved off the question. "Job satisfaction, happy investors, future considerations."

"A bonus?" I cocked my head towards Greenwood.

He held out his hand, swivelling it up and down. "Future prospects."

"What did you have to do for it?" I watched his face.

Greenwood tightened the belt on his bathrobe. "Renovate."

"Renovate?"

"Clean out the tenants."

"By when?"

"April Fool's Day"

"I see." I stared at Greenwood's bare toes. "So you didn't make it then?"

Greenwood scratched the stubble on his chin. "Nope."

I wrapped my arms around my body. "Tell me something, Digger. Who found Norman's body? The fire fighters?"

"Yeah."

"You had a false alarm on the day he died?"

"Yeah."

"So, he must have died not long before they found him?"

Greenwood shrugged and turned back to the glories of the morning. The sky was clear and the air smelled sweet and clean like it always did in the hours after a shower. After a few seconds, he glanced my way. "You have problems with how we run our business, Regina?"

"I sure do." Greenwood threw me one of his crooked smiles, but I looked away into the distance where the lights of the business district were paling against the morning sky. When he tried putting an arm around me, I shrank from his touch.

"I'm entitled to make a bloody living, comrade."

"A living, not a killing, Mr. Greenwood."

"Who's the killer, me?"

"You and Queenie, with individual contributions from the horticultural death squad: Rose, Bud, Lily, Herb and Fern. But most of all, you."

"Me?" Greenwood straightened up. "Lighten up, woman. How can you believe that I killed anybody. I'm an accountant."

"Yes, you," I said pointing my finger at his face. "'I'll tell you a story--a story about a loser named Norman Water. You let Norman into the hotel. You gave him an apartment. You let him charge meals to his room, and when he went over his credit limit, you gave him a job. But the lousy pay wouldn't even cover his hotel bills, much less what Fern and Queenie milked from him for counterfeit kisses or what Lily or Rose picked out of his pockets. At least Queenie said she was sorry."

"Woman, you don't have a clue what's really going on in the world."

"You watched as he went deeper and deeper in the hole. You sucked him dry. When he fought back with his childish practical jokes, you demoted him, then you fired him. When the owners decided to convert the place into a hotel, you tried evicting him, and when he refused to leave, you took his furniture."

"I didn't do that. Queenie did that."

"You even took away his clothes."

"That was Rose's doing--when he wouldn't let her room with him."

"You cut off his heat and his electricity. When that didn't work, you took his phone and turned off his water. You tried forcing him out of his little room. You figured you'd make things so uncomfortable he'd get out and quit. But he had nowhere else to go, so he hung in there. You didn't get anyone to help him, you simply left him to die."

The man threw me a knowing look. "Are you sure about that?"

"Isn't that what the naive bleeding-heart leftie Regina was supposed to believe?"

Greenwood scowled.

"Even if you didn't do everything yourself, you're still accountable, Mr. Accountant. You're the boss."

Greenwood affected a nonchalant pose. "You got it all wrong, woman."

"That's why you finally let me into the hotel, isn't it? You didn't give a damn about the Human Rights Commission. When I started asking about Norman Water, you knew I didn't know anything." My voice was straining against fatigue.

"You got that right," Greenwood jeered.

"You might as well have buried him alive, because you let him slowly die of starvation and thirst. You cold-hearted bastards wouldn't even let him have a glass of water--a glass of water, something that is free for the taking to anyone who can turn a tap. Even the homeless on the street can get a drink of water. Screw the money! You were never going to collect."

"It's not the bloody money. Winning is the thing. I told you, money is a just way of keeping score. Besides, he didn't want to go."

"You're crazy, Digger. Mean and crazy. You've had it in the hotel business."

Greenwood shrugged. "Business is business."

"Guys like you give crooks a bad name." I stole a peek at the driveway and parking lot down below. But feeling gravity's tug on the vagus nerve in my stomach, I turned away from the rail. Looking back towards the balcony door, I studied the frame around the glass.

"Water was a washout. He ruined everything he touched. Everything!"

"You killed him as dead as if you had used a bullet or a knife, and you know it."

"You know better than that, Reggie."

"No, I don't, Digger," I said. "Tell me about all the little rackets going on in your toxic enterprise. Don't tell me you didn't know what was going on right under your own nose?"

"That kind of stuff goes on in every hotel. I'm sorry about what happened to the kid. And I'll take some responsibility. This is a business not a charity but we should have taken care of Norman. We were not trying to deliberately starve him out. It was an accident and can be explained to the authorities. But please, Regina, please don't you pretend that you don't know why we had to force Norman out."

"Force him out?"

Digger shrugged. Having got the half-hearted apology off his chest, he was now totally relaxed. "Sure."

"Out?"

"Sure."

I took a beat to take in the city skyline. A car was turning around in the parking lot below. I watched it drive off, then got right into Greenwood's face. "Digger, you were <u>not</u>trying to force him out. You may have started to do that but, in the end, you were <u>not</u>trying to evict him."

"What?'

"I had it all wrong before. I was just trying out one story on you. Now let me tell you another story, a story about winners."

"Winners? Good. My kind of people."

"Yes, winners."

"Go on."

"Norman Water was your prisoner."

"You're out of your mind."

"I know why you couldn't let him go. He'd discovered your secret. He knew about your really big deal, didn't he?"

Greenwood tensed and gave me a guilty look. "No."

"It was not about business at all, it was about politics. It was not only about money, it was also about power--power and keeping the winners winning."

He looked hard at me for a moment before he made his move, then he grabbed at me. But, before he could get his hands on me, I jumped back into the hotel room and slammed the sliding door shut. Then I locked it, leaving Greenwood out on the balcony, half-blind and clad only in his bathrobe.

Greenwood stuck his nose on the glass. "You're leaving?"

"Yes."

Tapping on the glass, Greenwood yelled. "What about me? I'll freeze my buns out here!"

I approached the glass for one last word. "Greenwood, I don't want any more anonymous phone calls. Okay?"

His mouth opened and closed, like a puppet. Then he started pleading. "Oh come on, Regina. Can't you take a joke? Don't you care what happens to me? I'm a constituent. If you're not nice to me, I might have to run against you. And I've got lots juicy stuff to tell the voters. You know, I think I could beat you. You only had a majority of thirty-one votes. Thirty-one votes are nothing. Nothing!"

The fire alarm stopped and, a second later, so did the sprinklers. Through the open doorway to the hall, I heard the twang of an elevator cable.

Greenwood hammered at the glass and shrieked like a lunatic. "Regina! Help! Help!"

I watched for a minute, but seeing Greenwood trapped behind the glass gave me joy. What I needed to do now was phone Moss.

Hearing a cough behind me, I turned. There in the doorway, with a full-length duster coat draped over his shoulders, stood a figure from my working life. I stepped aside and waved the man in. "Mr. Minister, welcome to the Apartment Hotel. I wondered when you might come by"

"Oh, why's that?"

"As the political minister for this city, you're in charge of patronage and..."

"And?'

"Election preparations, and the like."

The Honourable Daniel D. Lyon did a quick double take at seeing

Greenwood out on the balcony before turning to give a quick dismissive glance at my damp hair and the disarray of my clothing. He took a deep breath, switched off his cell phone and slipped it into his raincoat pocket. He nodded at me and switched on his professional politician's voice. "We have to talk."

"What about?"

"About? About an unfortunate death, misunderstandings and political secrets."

"You threatening me, Minister?"

"Whoa." Lyon held up his hands. "We need to understand each other. The police will be here soon, and we should get a few things straight."

"Such as?" I sat down on Greenwood's bed.

Lyon sat down on the other side and very casually crossed his legs. Lowering his voice to a whisper, he said, "Do you have any idea what's been happening here?"

"I figured it out, yeah."

"And what do you think it is?"

"You want my seat."

"Yes."

"And more."

"More."

"Much more."

"Much?"

"It looks to me an awful lot like an old-fashioned gerrymander--a giant, world-class gerrymander--redrawing the city's electoral boundaries so they favour only your party."

Lyon was taken aback. "And what's the basis for this charge?"

"I found the numbers. Here in the hotel."

"Did you?"

"And the numbers are still here for all to see."

Lyon looked appalled. "They are?"

"Yes, sir, but I don't know why."

"Because you won a squeaker at the last election..."

"Yes?"

"...you probably think the conservative seats are all as safe as houses."

"Probably."

"Well, we do lots of polling and the long term trends are pretty iffy."

"Iffy? That's news to me--good news--but news just the same."

"Naturally, we have a different perspective."

"Naturally. So you planned to push all the low income, anti-Tory voters out of the district so that I'd lose my seat."

"Right. We could be in deep manure at the next one. We need a big break."

"But it's not just my seat you're after."

"No."

"Hightucker's too."

"No, not Hightucker. We're going to make that the safest district in the city."

"No!"

"Yes."

"How? No, don't tell me."

"You'll never guess."

"You're after all my party's inner-city seats, except that one. Your idea is to pack my friend Hightucker's district with as many public housing units and emergency shelters as money could buy."

Lyon grinned. "Right. Your crowd could never object to that, and we'd hive all those left-wing votes into just one area."

"But first you had to squeeze all sorts of marginal folk out of all the neighbouring districts, including mine. Then, you'd get a tame boundary commission to redraw the boundary lines to give all your bad polls to Hightucker"

"And all the city's good polls to our team."

"God, Lyon, there's got to be a name for that."

"The Ontario Tories used to call it 'hiving the grits."

"I was thinking 'electoral fraud.' The NDP would get one super-safe seat, and you guys would get all the rest."

"Most of them anyway. At least that's the plan."

"And your accountant buddy out there on the balcony did all the arithmetic?"

"He volunteered for the assignment."

"And Norman Water figured out what was going on."

"It seems that way."

"So he was just a casualty in the political wars?"

Lyon stood. "Collateral damage. As I found from a recent phone conversation with our friend Greenwood, his crew had the boy under a form of house arrest."

"You freely admit it? God, Lyon, surely seats in the Legislature are nothing to kill for."

"No, but a whole government, that's very tempting." Lyon gave a weary laugh then, seeing the look on my face, bit it short. "No, it's not. I swear it: Nobody in the administration ever heard of Norman 'til he died. Digger and his people went too far. Way too far. I guess Digger got a little ambitious. A fanatic, you might say."

"Fanatic is right. But I'm sure he's very good at what he does for you."

"I suppose."

"I suppose you bastards are totally nuts. Were you really going to run Digger Greenwood as a candidate? Against me?"

"We've done worse."

"No kidding. Look, you know I'm going to tell the police everything."

"I expect no less from you." Lyon stood up to brush water off the cuffs of his pants, the political smoothie back in the saddle. "I just want you to know that neither the government nor myself had anything to do with Digger's dirty work."

"But your friend did kill Norman?"

"Everybody did it, and nobody. They'll probably never convict anyone."

"Yeah? What about the gerrymander? That'll be a huge scandal."

"There's nothing illegal about a gerrymander."

"Maybe not, but you're a provincial cabinet minister. It is totally unethical. You cannot pass that buck."

"Of course not. I'll probably have to resign--for a while. No big deal. I'll be back in no time."

"I'd bet money on it. But why go to all the trouble?"

"You already know the answer to that question, Regina."

I stared at Lyon, uncomprehending. Then I looked at the floor and it hit me. "Water?"

"Water. See. You're smarter than you look Regina Colwell."

"Privatization."

"We need an unstoppable majority, a landslide."

"To privatize the municipal water systems?"

"Plus the electric utility and anything else we can unload"

"I was joking!"

"No joke, I assure you. It's good public policy. Getting government off the backs of the people."

"So you're going to give the good people of the city competing privately owned water works? And competing sewer lines running side by side?"

"No, there'd be a private monopoly but first we'd invite tenders."

"That makes me feel so much better."

"In future, money will flow with the water."

"So, Evian is the issue."

The minister chortled. "Sure, that puts it very well."

"Thanks." I searched Lyon's face for any sign that he saw anything wrong with his plan but there was none. He had privileged me with a glimpse into the future and now he was done with me.

Lyon glanced at the man shivering on the balcony. Greenwood was now crouched in the corner, waiting--a bit like Norman Water during his worst days in 505. "Now, if you don't mind, I'd like a word with

Digger."

"He's all yours."

Lyon fumbled with the lock on the glass door and pulled it back. He stood at the opening, slowly shaking his head at Greenwood.

Water leaked from the hallway through the room's carpet out onto the balcony and over the ledge. Greenwood's feet started to get wet and, in a display of bravado, he hopped up onto the balcony rail. As the water ran off the balcony, Greenwood sat with his bare bottom balanced on the metal rail, teetering dangerously but grinning like a lottery winner.

Lyon looked back and dismissed me with a little bow. He waited for me to depart, then he turned towards Greenwood. I glanced back and saw a gust of wind lift the flaps of the minister's coat and Greenwood blindly grinning at Lyon. Then I headed across the now sodden carpet towards the hallway door.

"You've been a complete idiot, Digger." I heard Lyon snarl.

"No way!" Greenwood shouted

I heard the shout and spun around but he was already gone. Where Digger Greenwood had been only a moment before was just an empty space. Minister Lyon turned to me with a horrified look but I simply bolted out the door.

Out front, the ambulance attendants were loading Greenwood's body onto a stretcher. A constable with a notebook asked me if I had seen the man fall. I shook my head.

Water dripped from the lobby ceiling tiles onto the carpet below. I closed my eyes and saw it seeping through the carpet and out the door onto the street, trickling into the gutters, flushing the storm sewers, flooding the river, drifting out to sea to land on a hot beach, where it would evaporate under the sun, rise up to the heavens, then, as clouds, fly back to the land, the mountains and plains, to fall as snow and rain again--an infinite second coming, fuelling the never-ending cycle of economic life, and political death. Damn, I though, I've got to stop making speeches to myself!

I picked up the lobby pay phone and dialled my home number. "Moss, I'm only going to say this once. So, here's the deal. Trade places with me--you can have my hotel room--and I'll give you the scoop of your life. Norman Water didn't drown, he died of dehydration. And Norman had a discovered a big political secret, something truly scandalous. If you want to know all the dirty details, pack your bags and meet me here in half an hour. Okay?"

"Okay, but, man oh man, what is going on down there? Regina?"

"Lyon and the boys were trying to steal the next election with a rigged constituency boundaries commission, and Norman Water found out about it."

"I don't understand what that had to do with the hotel."

"Greenwood was their number cruncher. And their candidate against me."

"Do you think I could get an interview with him?"

"No, Moss, he's dead. He fell out of the building. You might say he was the fall guy."

"Man! I'll get there as quick as I can."

"Think syndication, Moss, banner headlines and newspaper awards."

I hung up and sat down in the lobby to wait until I could go home to my own bed.

# EPILOGUE

Monday, April 3

Monday's headlines were all screamers. The page-one banners in the morning paper read: "Political fixer dead; Coroner investigates," "Regina reads writing on the wall" and "Lyon resigns." Inside on page two were three articles: "Greenwood a fanatic, Lyon claims" "Lyon blames Colwell for impeding investigation" and "MLA mourns informant." Of course, none of them got the whole story. Few of the reporters had it even half right. Moss did well but his front-page copy was heavily edited by his newspapers editors and lawyers. Nevertheless, over the coming week most of the major facts slowly became public.

From the day he checked into the hotel, things had gone downhill for Norman Water. Digger Greenwood ran The Apartment Hotel like a company store. If he could get his staff eating his restaurant's food and renting his rooms, then he counted that as a huge saving. If they got into debt, they became practically his slaves. Norman had worked his way down from the front desk to the back stairs to a cold and empty room. As he descended into Apartment Hotel hell, he fought back with practical jokes but these only aggravated his situation. By then he could not easily leave because Rose had taken all his clothes.

When he had no more money, Greenwood tried to force him out by cutting off his heat, light and water. To get something to drink, Norman set off the sprinklers. While he was still working at the hotel, Norman found those numbers. And, afterwards, he figured out what they meant. When Queenie and Bud took away his wet furniture, they must have seen the numbers on the wall. After that, Greenwood the extremist figured he could not afford to let Norman go. Norman and Digger both knew the gerrymander was wrong. Both probably figured it was illegal, a serious crime, but both were wrong. Now, both were dead.

From the moment Queenie and Bud discovered Norman with the poll numbers, he became the hotel's prisoner and Greenwood was apparently prepared to starve him into silence. But Norman had kept one little box of matches. Last week, in desperation, he set off the fire alarms and sprinklers again. This time, the fire fighters came but it was too late. Shortly before they arrived, Norman died of dehydration.

I read all the Monday morning stories over coffee in the legislative cafeteria. At nine, I had an appointment with Dr. Corbeau. This time, he was coming to see me. But before that I had to deal with a constituent. The Apartment Hotel was closed because of water damage and Bud Budinski wanted me to help him get a new job.

Made in the USA
Lexington, KY
21 April 2015